Keyboarding Course

Microsoft® Word 2010

Susie H. VanHuss, Ph.D.
Distinguished Professor Emeritus
University of South Carolina

Connie M. Forde, Ph.D.
Mississippi State University

Donna L. Woo
Cypress College, California

SOUTH-WESTERN
CENGAGE Learning™

Australia • Brazil • Japan • Korea • Mexico • Singapore • Spain • United Kingdom • United States

SOUTH-WESTERN
CENGAGE Learning™

Keyboarding Course, Lessons 1–25, Eighteenth Edition

Susie H. VanHuss, Connie M. Forde, Donna L. Woo

Vice President of Editorial, Business: Jack W. Calhoun

Vice President/Editor-in-Chief: Karen Schmohe

Vice President/Marketing: Bill Hendee

Sr. Acquisitions Editor: Jane Phelan

Sr. Developmental Editor: Dave Lafferty

Consulting Editors: Catherine Skintik; Mary Todd, Todd Publishing Services

Editorial Assistant: Conor Allen

Associate Marketing Manager: Shanna Shelton

Sr. Content Project Manager: Martha Conway

Sr. Media Editor: Mike Jackson

Sr. Print Buyer: Charlene Taylor

Production Service: PreMedia Global

Copyeditor: Gary Morris

Sr. Art Director: Tippy McIntosh

Internal Designer: Grannan Design, Ltd.

Cover Designer: Grannan Design, Ltd.

Cover Image: © Markus Dziable, iStock: © penfold, iStock; illustration, Grannan Design, Ltd.

Sr. Rights Specialist, Photos: Deanna Ettinger

Photo Researcher: Bill Smith Group

Sr. Rights Specialist, Text: Mardell Glinski Schultz

Student Edition ISBN-13: 978-0-538-49539-4
Student Edition ISBN 10: 0-538-49539-1

Student Edition with Keyboarding Pro 6 CD
ISBN-13: 978-1-111-42646-0
Student Edition with Keyboarding Pro 6 CD
ISBN-10: 1-111-42646-5

South-Western Cengage Learning
5191 Natorp Boulevard
Mason, OH 45040
USA

Cengage Learning products are represented in Canada by
Nelson Education, Ltd.

For your course and learning solutions, visit **www.cengage.com/highered**
Visit our company website at **www.cengage.com**

Printed in the United States of America
1 2 3 4 5 6 7 14 13 12 11 10

Contents

It Keeps Getting Better

College Keyboarding solutions have a track record of ensuring success, and they just keep getting better. You can rely on the new *18th edition* to provide print and digital solutions that work for you.

Tools that Work: Integrated Textbook, Software, Web

Lessons Plus Meaningful Applications

The *Keyboarding Course* includes 25 lessons, numerous extra pages of drills and timed writings, and rich applications for applying new skills. **NEW** Part 2 applies web computing activities for the Internet, Cloud computing, and Web 2.0, as well as communication, numeric keypad and word processing applications.

Keyboarding Pro 6: Your KEY to Success

Keyboarding Pro 6 helps you build the skills needed to meet the challenges of the digital workplace. It's engaging, interactive, easy to navigate, and provides motivating, instant feedback. **NEW:** *Keyboarding Pro 6* now includes those basic communication skills needed in the workplace.

Web Reporter for In-Class or Online Courses

Online courses just got easier with Web Reporter. Students use their browser to send instructors assignments. Instructors can manage their classes, view documents, and utilize the gradebook–all online.

Reliable, Dependable, Easy to Use

Correct techniques, an abundance of crafted drills, and a variety of meaningful routines keep lessons fun and build skill. Both the textbook lessons and software work together to teach the new keys, reinforce proper reaches, emphasize technique, encourage accuracy, and build fluency.

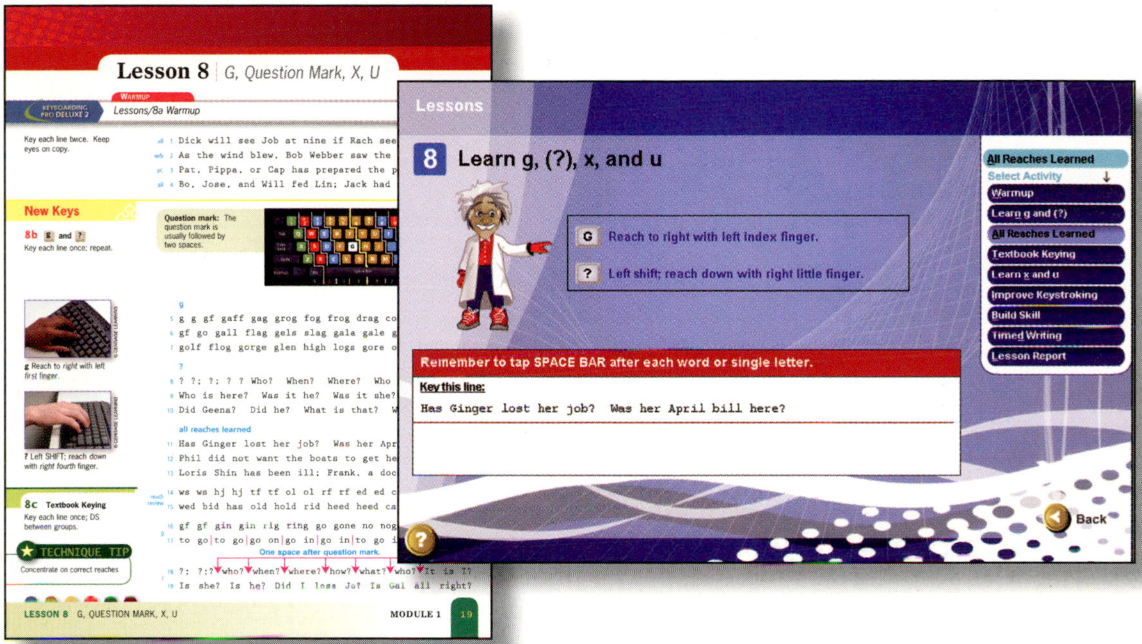

Extra Practice Builds Confidence and Success

An **additional 20 lessons** in *Keyboarding Pro 6* will challenge you to improve at every level. **Technique Drills** and **Quick Review** provide extra practice to strengthen accuracy and techniques.

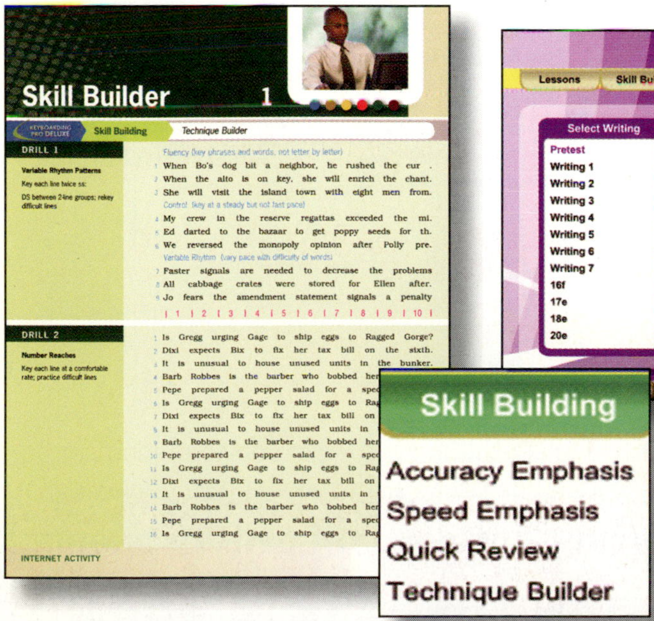

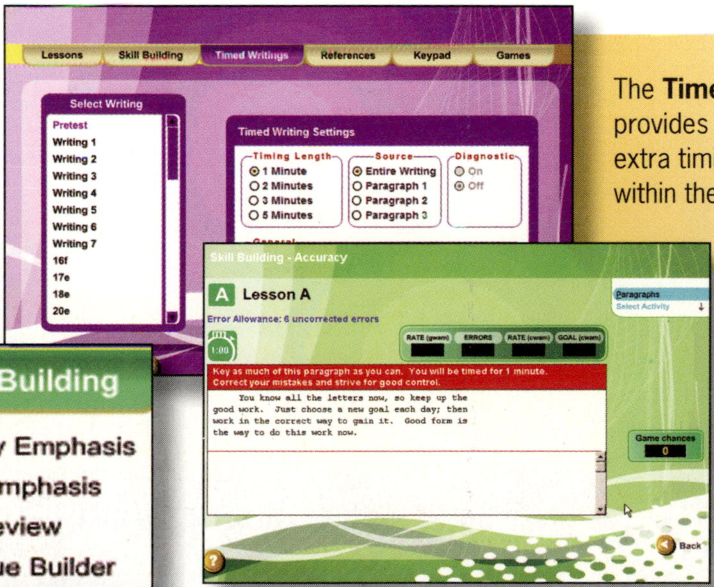

The **Timed Writings** tab provides quick access to many extra timings beyond those within the lessons.

Always Fresh, Always New

Numeric Keypad Practice and Timed Writings Build Skill.

Keyboarding Pro 6 teaches the Keypad and provides Keypad Timed Writings and Practice. The textbook provides extra drills to build skill.

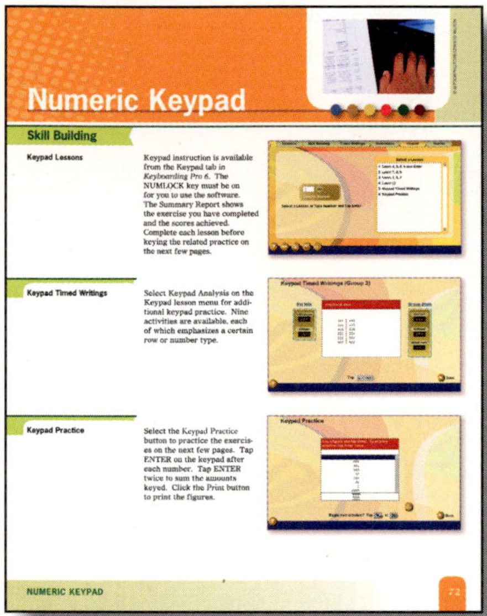

Communication Skills Integrated

Proofreading, spelling, composition, subject/verb agreement and other activities apply the **communication activities** introduced in *Keyboarding Pro 6*.

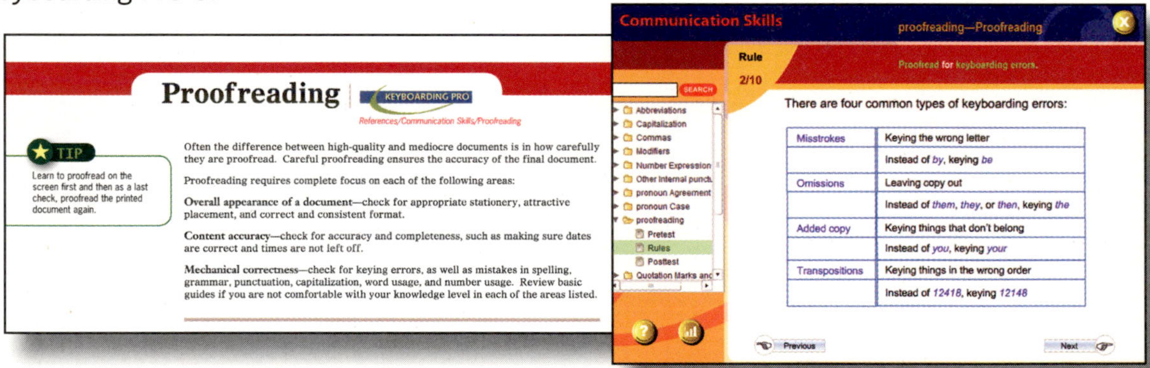

NEW! Web-Based Computing

Internet, Cloud, and Web 2.0 are key components of web-based computing; easy to use activities help students learn and apply the basics.

Word Processing Basics Simple word processing applications, including composition activities and personal business letter format, give you an opportunity to use your skills in a practical way. The word processor has a timer for classroom instruction.

Reference Guide Enhanced: Hot topics such as *Windows 7* and File Management, Digital Citizenship, Technology and Your Health are included to keep you up to date on Keyboarding and your future.

College Keyboarding 18e: It Keeps Getting Better

One Series: the Right Number of Lessons

Make your life easier with proven textbooks and software that have the appropriate number of lessons for today's course. Plenty of documents and a strong instructional model combine to build confidence and proficiency in keyboarding, formatting, and word processing skills. The **new 18th edition** merges the strengths of the *Essentials* series and the efficiencies of the *Certified Approach.*

Keyboarding and Word Processing Essentials, 18e, Lessons 1-55
(978-0-538-495387)
Master the keyboarding and formatting skills most important for career success, including formatting business documents with *Microsoft® Word 2010.*

Advanced Word Processing, 18e, Lessons 56-110
(978-0-538-49540-0)
Ten modules emphasize memos and letters, advanced reports, mail merge, graphics, meeting documents, medical and legal documents, employment documents with advanced word processing commands. Includes two comprehensive projects.

Keyboarding and Word Processing, Complete Course, 18e, Lessons 1-120
(978-0-538-49647-6)
The *Complete Course* adds 10 additional lessons with topics for certification.

Keyboarding Pro DELUXE 2
Student License (978-0-840-05335-0)
Keyboarding Pro DELUXE 2 now checks document formats and fully supports Lessons 1-110.

To Our Teachers and Students

Thank you for choosing our keyboarding materials. We have designed them to make it easy to teach and learn keyboarding, formatting, and *Word 2010* skills. We hope they meet your needs and wish you much success in developing these valuable career skills.

Your College Keyboarding authors

Susie VanHuss Connie Forde Donna Woo

Technology Tools Working for You

You are about to tap into the best print and digital tools available for keyboarding. Quite simply, South-Western's tools have prepared thousands of students for success in school and beyond. Following is a brief discussion of the technology tools for use with *College Keyboarding 18e, Lessons 1–25:*

- *Keyboarding Pro 6*
- *Web Reporter*
- *Website Resources*
- *E-mail*

KEYBOARDING PRO 6

Keyboarding Pro 6 is the perfect companion for either online or in-class keyboarding instruction. This all-in-one keyboarding software is compatible with *Windows 7, Windows Vista, or Windows XP.*

MAIN MENU

The Main menu includes the primary tabs to use the software and navigation buttons to execute common commands. Each tab is briefly described below.

Lessons: Lessons 1–25 teach the keys and build skill on the keyboard. You will see demonstrations of correct techniques and practice at least five different types of drills that are fun and keep you motivated. Drills are keyed both from the screen and from the textbook. A red checkmark appears after the lesson name when it is a completed lesson.

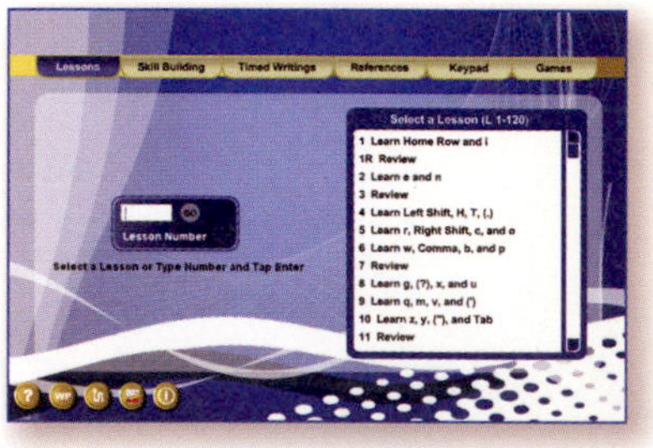

Skill Building As soon as you know the alphabetic reaches, use the 20 accuracy or speed lessons to build fluency; use these lessons any time after Lesson 10. Use **Technique Builder** to practice the drills found in Skill Builders 1–3 in the textbook and **Quick Check** to practice various reaches. Results of these exercises are shown on the Skill Building Report.

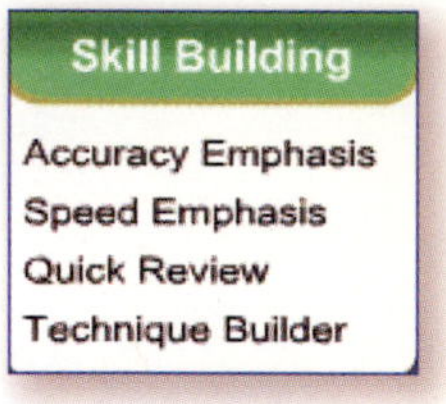

Timed Writings Easy access to all timings is available from the Timed Writings tab as well as from the lessons in which they appear. Your 3–5 best and last 40 timings are reported on the Timed Writing Report.

References **Communication Skills** review eight common language arts topics; each includes a pretest, posttest, rules, examples, and exercises to check understanding. **Tutorial videos** teach you to transfer your student record and troubleshoot issues.

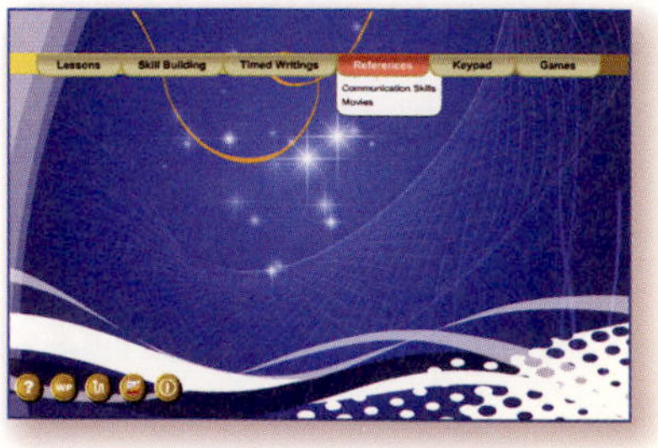

Keypad You will learn the numeric keypad by touch and build your skill. Timed writings build skill. Results for Keypad lessons are shown on the Summary Lessons 1–25 report.

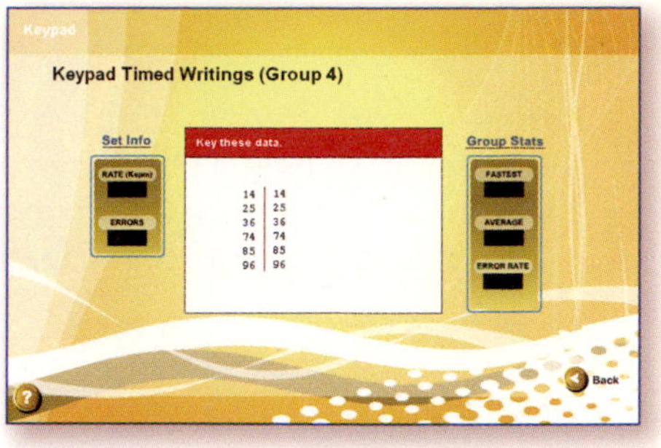

Navigation: The navigation buttons at the bottom of the Main menu execute common commands. Roll over the buttons with your mouse to identify their purpose.

GET STARTED

Launch *Keyboarding Pro 6*: From the Start menu, select Programs, then South-Western Keyboarding, and click *Keyboarding Pro 6 (or Keyboarding Pro DELUXE 2).*

Create your student record (one time only). The student record reflects your work.

1. Select **New User** from the Login screen.
2. Complete the required fields. Record your security question and answer in a safe location. You will need this information to login to Web Reporter.

Non-distance learning class: Select your class from the Class drop-down menu. Ignore Class Code. If you are creating the student record on a **flash drive**, see the *User's Guide* for instruction. Subsequently when logging in, select your name from the Log In screen and key your password. If you do not see your name, click the Folder icon; browse to locate your student record.

Distance learning class: Leave the Class field empty.

- Locate the document provided by your instructor with the **Class Code**.
- Double-click the Class Code to select it. Right click the Class Code and choose *Copy*.
- Toggle (ALT + TAB) to the New Student dialog box and paste the Class Code in the Class Code field. To paste, right click in the Class Code field, and choose *Paste*.
- Click OK. The software will issue a **Student ID**. Copy and paste this to the document from your instructor with the Class Code. You will need both of these codes in order to download your file to another computer.

If you create your student record at school, you will need to download it to your home computer. Do NOT create a second student record.

To download your student record to your home computer: Click **Locate Online Student** from the Login screen and copy/paste in your Class Code and Student ID. This is a one-time process. (*See User's Manual.*)

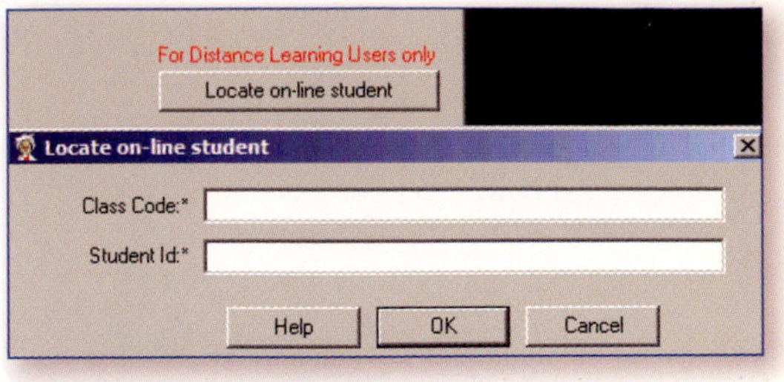

3. Transfer your student record to the Web Reporter or flash drive if you will be working from home or another location. See the videos under References for details.
   - To transfer your student record to a flash drive, use the Export command.
   - To transfer your file using Web Reporter, select Yes when logging out to upload your work to Web Reporter.

REPORTS

Numerous reports are available from the Reports option on the menu bar. Each lesson report hyperlinks to a specific lesson. Instructors can view these same reports in Web Reporter or the Instructor Utility.

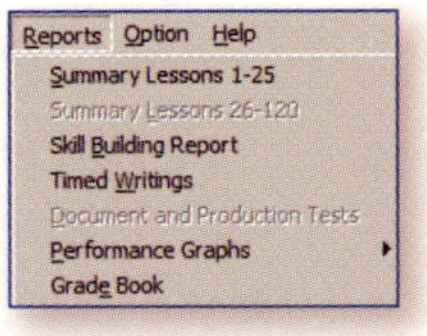

Web Reporter

Web Reporter is an easy solution for online users to send assignments to the instructor. The relationship with the Web Reporter is established when you create your student record and paste in the Class Code. For best results when using Web Reporter, use a direct connection to the Web rather than a wireless connection. The quality of wireless service can vary wildly from one Internet Service Provider to another.

To access Web Reporter, enter your user name, password, security question and answer, and e-mail.

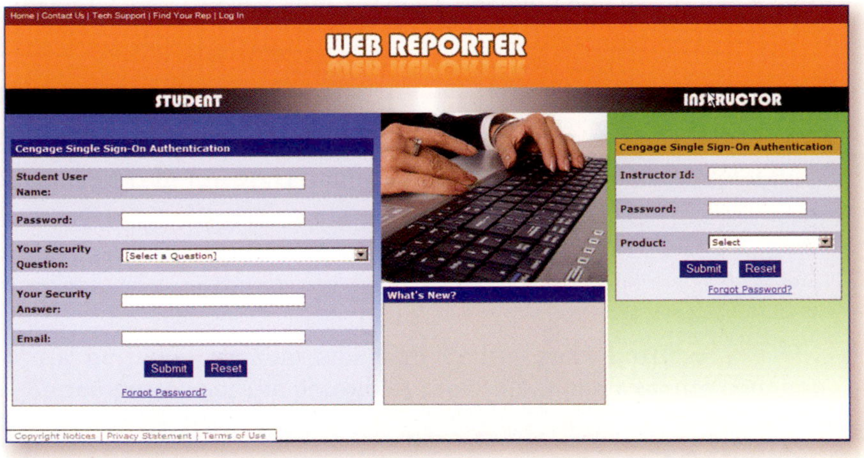

Web Resources www.collegekeyboarding.com

The website has several resources to enrich your experience. From the website www.collegekeyboarding.com, choose *College Keyboarding 18e*, and then choose *Keyboarding Course Lessons 1–25*. These chapter resources are also available as a ***WebTutor Toolbox*** for use with Blackboard or other learning management systems.

ELECTRONIC MAIL

Electronic mail (or **e-mail**) is a message sent by one computer user to another. E-mail was originally designed as an informal, personal way of communicating. However, it is now used extensively in business. For business use, e-mail should not be casual or informal.

Business writers compose e-mail messages in two ways. First, the writer may compose the entire communication (or message) in the body of the e-mail. Second, the writer may compose a brief e-mail message and then attach electronic documents to it. Distribution of electronic documents via e-mail is a common business practice; these documents include many types of document formats, e.g., memos, letters, reports, contracts, worksheets, and presentations. It is important for the business writer to recognize the importance of attractive and acceptable formats of all documents, including e-mail messages.

Using e-mail requires an e-mail program, an e-mail address, and access to the Internet.

Address e-mail carefully. Key and check the address of the recipient, and always supply a subject line. Also, key the e-mail address of anyone who should receive a copy of the e-mail.

Format the body of an e-mail single-spaced; double-space between paragraphs. Do not indent paragraphs. Limit the use of bold, italics, and uppercase. For business use, avoid abbreviations and emoticons (e.g., BTW for *by the way* or ;- for wink).

Attach electronic documents to an e-mail message using the attachment feature of the e-mail program. The attached file can then be opened and edited by the recipient.

CREATE AN E-MAIL ACCOUNT

If you do not have an e-mail account, several companies provide free e-mail service. The following directions can be used to create a Hotmail account:

1. Use an Internet browser to go to *www.hotmail.com*.
2. If you do not have a Hotmail account, click the Sign up button and key the information to set up your e-mail account.

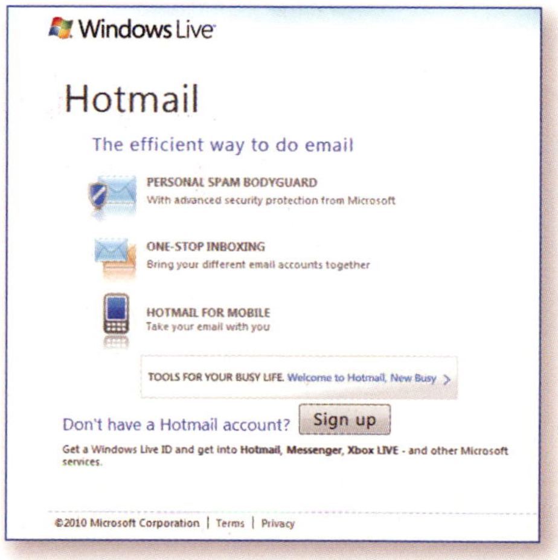

Know Your Computer

The numbered parts are found on most computers. The location of some parts will vary.

1. **CPU** (**Central Processing Unit):** Internal operating unit or "brain" of computer.
2. **CD-ROM drive:** Reads data from and writes data to a CD or DVD.
3. **Monitor:** Displays text and graphics on a screen.
4. **Mouse:** Used to input commands.
5. **Keyboard:** An arrangement of letter, figure, symbol, control, function, and editing keys and a numeric keypad.

KEYBOARD ARRANGEMENT

1. **Alphanumeric keys:** Letters, numbers, and symbols.
2. **Numeric keypad:** Keys at the right side of the keyboard used to enter numeric copy and perform calculations.
3. **Function (F) keys:** Used to execute commands, sometimes with other keys. Commands vary with software.
4. **Arrow keys:** Move insertion point up, down, left, or right.
5. **ESC (Escape):** Closes a software menu or dialog box.
6. **TAB:** Moves the insertion point to a preset position.
7. **CAPS LOCK:** Used to make all capital letters.
8. **SHIFT:** Makes capital letters and symbols shown at tops of number keys.
9. **CTRL (Control):** With other key(s), executes commands. Commands may vary with software.
10. **ALT (Alternate):** With other key(s), executes commands. Commands may vary with software.
11. **Space Bar:** Inserts a space in text.
12. **ENTER (return):** Moves insertion point to margin and down to next line. Also used to execute commands.
13. **DELETE:** Removes text to the right of insertion point.
14. **NUM LOCK:** Activates/deactivates numeric keypad.
15. **INSERT:** Activates insert or typeover.
16. **BACKSPACE:** Deletes text to the left of insertion point.

Level 1

DEVELOPING KEYBOARDING SKILL

Learning Outcomes

Keyboarding

- To key the alphabetic and numeric keys by touch.
- To develop good keyboarding techniques.
- To key fluently—at least 25 words per minute.
- To develop reasonable accuracy.

Communication Skills

- To develop proofreading skills.
- To apply proofreaders' marks and revise text.

Web-Based Computing 3 | Web 2.0

WEB 2.0

Most people think of the first generation of the Internet as a vast online collection of information that can be accessed easily and at little or no cost. The role of the Internet user is simply to access information in a passive way for whatever purpose the user needs the information. Most people think of the second generation of the Internet (Web 2.0) as an interactive tool that enables the user to contribute and collaborate with others. The role of the Web 2.0 user is that of an active participant. Web 2.0 applications are often thought of as social networking.

SOCIAL MEDIA TOOLS

Many options exist that enable Web 2.0 users to participate actively. The group of social media tools listed below is one way of looking at just a few of the different options available to users who want to participate actively in the second generation of the Internet.

Social networks are generally thought of as tools for sharing information with an online community of people with common interests. Facebook, LinkedIn, and MySpace are examples of frequently used social networks.

Micro-blogging sites enable users to send brief messages (often 140 or fewer characters) to a group of people which in turn can be sent to other groups. Twitter and Tumblr are examples of micro-blogging sites.

Video sharing sites provide a platform for people to post videos to share with others. YouTube, Metacafe, Break, and Google Video are examples of video-sharing sites.

Photo sharing sites provide a platform for people to post photographs to share with others. Examples include Flickr, Photobucket, Webshots, and Fotki.

Blogs are sites that provide publishing tools for people to post articles and various types of information to share with others and accept comments from readers. Examples of blog hosting sites include Blogger from Google, WordPress, and Live Journal.

Bookmarking sites allow users to bookmark or tag sites that they recommend. Examples are Delicious, Furl, Reddit, and StumbleUpon.

DRILL 3

WEB 2.0

1. Search for one article in each of the categories using the name of the category shown in bold as the keywords. Use the article as the basis for deciding which site in that category you will visit.
2. In each category, visit the website of one of the examples of sites listed.
3. Select one site in any of the categories and contribute something to the site. Post a photo, video, a blog, or whatever you would like to post.

Keyboarding Assessment/Placement

KEYBOARDING PRO DELUXE 2

Warmup

Warmup

1. Open *Keyboarding Pro*.
2. Go to the Word Processor by clicking the WP.
3. Key each line twice. Tap ENTER after each group of lines.
4. Close the document by clicking X in the upper-right corner.

alphabet
1 Max quietly promised a very big gift for the jazz club next week.
2 Zack worked on five great projects and quickly became the expert.
3 Jack Meyer analyzed the data by answering five complex questions.

figures
4 The invoice dated 9/28/11 was for $17,493.56; it is due 10/24/11.
5 Our dinner on 6/25/11 cost $432.97 plus 18% tip totaling $510.90.
6 The 3 invoices (#49875, #52604, and #137986) totaled $379,912.46.

easy
7 Pam may go with me to town to work for the auditor if he is busy.
8 Jan and six girls may go to the lake to sit on the dock and fish.
9 My neighbor may tutor the eight girls on the theory and problems.

Timed Writing

1. From the main screen, click the Timed Writings tab.

   Timed Writings

2. Choose 3' as the length. Choose *pretest* from the list of writings.
3. Tap TAB to begin. Key from the textbook.
4. Repeat the timing for 3'.
5. Your results will be displayed in the Timed Writing Report, which is available on the menu bar.

LA ALL LETTERS

	gwam 1'	3'
Most businesses want to be seen as good citizens. Working with	13	4
the arts is one way in which they can give back to the community	26	9
in which they operate. It is easy to support the arts because most	39	13
people believe that a vibrant arts program is key to the quality of	53	18
life for local citizens. Quality of life is a major factor in recruiting	68	23
new employees.	71	24
Most art groups are nonprofits that provide tax benefits to those	13	28
who give to them. A business may give money, services, or products,	27	33
or it may sponsor an event. Sponsoring an event is not the same	40	37
as making a gift. The business receives a public relations benefit	54	42
by having its name linked with the event, whereas a gift may have	67	46
no obvious benefit. Both forms help the arts.	76	49
A business may also support the arts by buying and displaying	13	53
art in its facilities. Some choose to use the art of local artists, while	27	58
others buy high-quality art from well-known artists. The former	40	63
helps to build a good local art community. The latter may bring	53	67
recognition to the business for the quality of its artwork.	66	71

1' | 1 | 2 | 3 | 4 | 5 | 6 | 7 | 8 | 9 | 10 | 11 | 12 |
3' | 1 | 2 | 3 | 4 |

4. Select New or Add Files.

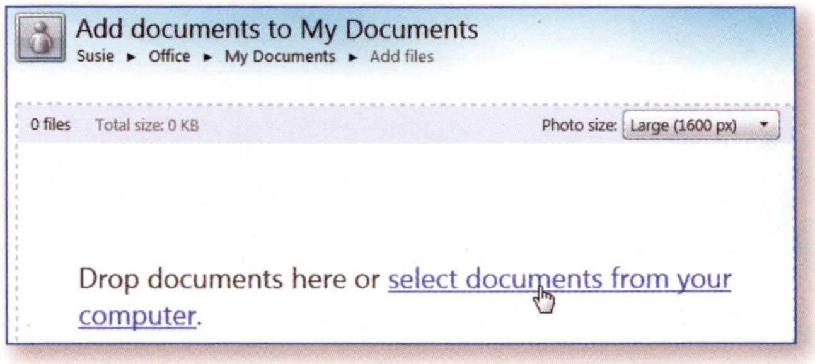

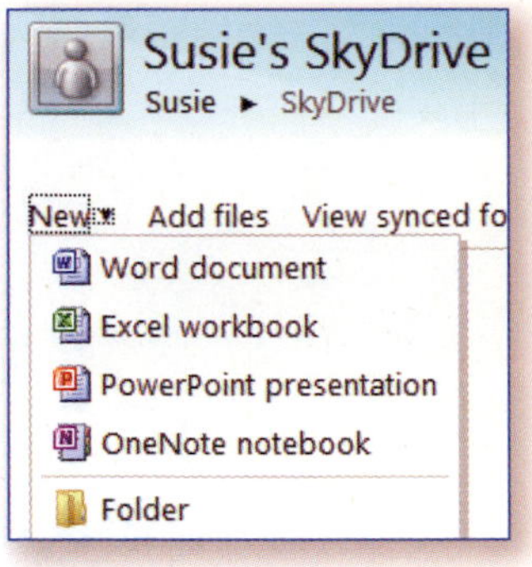

TIP

Note that when you view a document on the SkyDrive, it displays exactly like the one you created in WP Drill 9. Some formats are not available for documents created on the SkyDrive.

TIP

Many of the format commands are the same as the ones you used on the Keyboarding Pro Word Processor.

5. To add a file, click Add files and then select document from your computer.
6. Select the desired file and it uploads. Double-click the file name to open and view it.

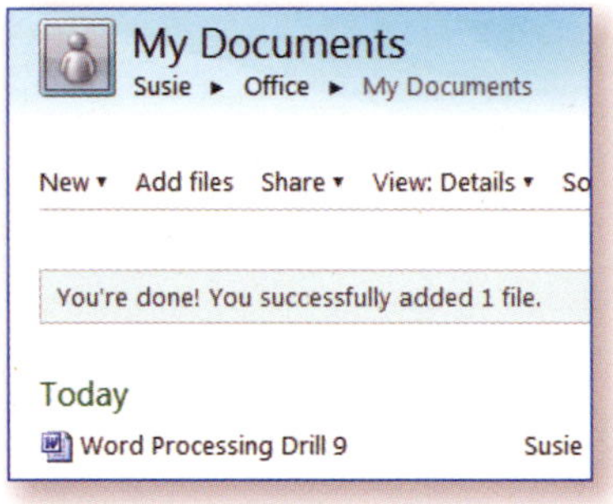

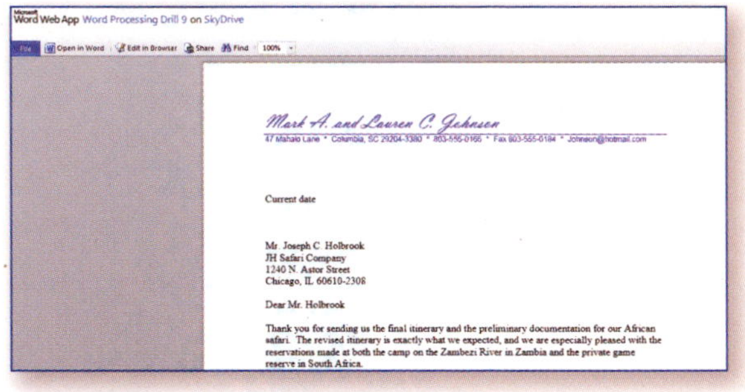

7. To create a document, click New and select Word document. (See illustration above). The Word ribbon and screen displays. Key the document name in the Name box and click Save. Then key and format the desired document.
8. Click File and select Save when you have finished; close and exit SkyDrive.

DRILL 2

WEB APPS

1. Create a new document. Key and format the document shown in the illustration below.
2. Save the document as *My First SkyDrive Doc*.

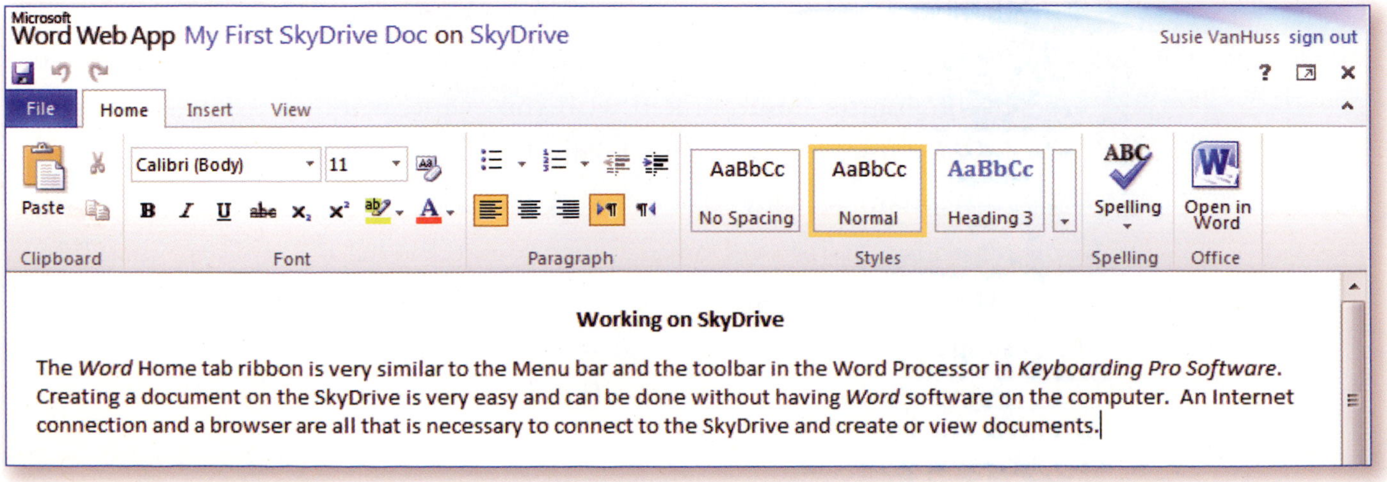

MODULE 1

Alphabetic Keys

Lessons 1–10 *Alphabetic and Basic Punctuation Keys*

Lessons 11–13 *Review*

LEARNING OUTCOMES

- Key the alphabetic keys by touch.
- Key using proper techniques.
- Key at a rate of 14 *gwam* or more.

Lesson 1 | *Home Row, Space Bar, Enter, I*

1a Home-Row Position and Space Bar

1. *Open Keyboarding Pro* and create your student record.
2. Go to the Word Processor. (The WP will appear next to exercises keyed in the Word Processor in Lessons 1–25.)
3. Practice the steps at the right until you can place your hands in home-row position without watching.
4. Key the drills at the bottom of the page several times.
5. Continue to the next page; keep the document on your screen.

HOME-ROW POSITION

1. Drop your hands to your side. Allow your fingers to curve naturally. Maintain this curve as you key.
2. Lightly place your left fingers over the **a s d f** and the right fingers over the **j k l ;**. You will feel a raised element on the *f* and *j* keys, which will help you keep your fingers on the home position. You are now in **home-row position**.

© CENGAGE LEARNING

SPACE BAR AND ENTER

Tap the Space Bar, located at the bottom of the keyboard, with a down-and-in motion of the right thumb to space between words.

© CENGAGE LEARNING

Enter Reach with the fourth (little) finger of the right hand to ENTER. Tap it to return the insertion point to the left margin. This action creates a **hard return**. Use a hard return at the end of all drill lines. Quickly return to home position (over ;).

© CENGAGE LEARNING

Key these lines

a s d f SPACE j k l ; ENTER

a s d f SPACE j k l ; ENTER

CLOUD COMPUTING

Cloud computing is an evolving concept and, as such, is very difficult to define. Cloud computing can be simplified by examining the following concepts involved in cloud computing:

- A cloud computing system consists of many high-powered computer resources, such as servers, networks, storage applications, software applications, and information technology (IT) services that can be easily accessed with a basic computer and an Internet connection.
- The resources can be accessed anytime, from any location, and without any involvement of the organization providing the services. An example would be Hotmail or Gmail from Google. They are Web-based, available on demand, and accomplished without interaction with the provider.
- The IT services provided to businesses are fee-based services. Some services may be provided free, such as *Google Docs* and *Microsoft Web Apps*. Both of these Web applications are also often referred to as Web 2.0 applications. Cloud computing serves as a bridge between the Internet and Web 2.0.

WEB-BASED E-MAIL

Information on creating an e-mail account is presented on page xi in the front part of your textbook. If you have not read that information, you should read the information carefully and set up a free Hotmail account before moving to the next section. If you have already set up the account and sent or received e-mail using it, you have used cloud computing. Your next venture into cloud computing will be to learn more about Web Apps.

WEB APPS

You keyed a document about Web Apps in Drill 8, p. 82 of the Word Processing section to help you learn about Web Apps. In this section, you will work with *Microsoft Web Apps* and learn how to view and to create a document on the SkyDrive. Your Hotmail e-mail address and your password serve as your *Windows Live*™ ID.

To access the SkyDrive and add or create a document:

www.windowslive.com

1. Sign in using your Hotmail address and Password.
2. Hover the mouse over Windows Live.
3. Click SkyDrive.

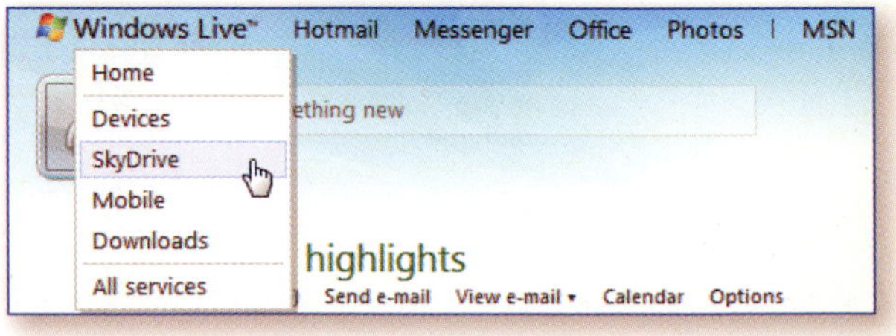

(continued)

New Keys

1b Procedures for Learning New Keys

Apply these steps each time you learn a new key.

STANDARD PLAN for Learning New Keyreaches

1. Find the new key on the illustrated keyboard. Then find it on your keyboard.
2. Watch your finger make the reach to the new key a few times. Keep other fingers curved in home position. For an upward reach, straighten the finger slightly; for a downward reach, curve the finger a bit more.
3. Repeat the drill until you can key it fluently.

1c Home Row

1. The Word Processor should be open.
2. Key lines 1–9 once. Tap ENTER once at the end of each line and twice to double-space (DS) between 2-line groups.
3. Keep the document on your screen.

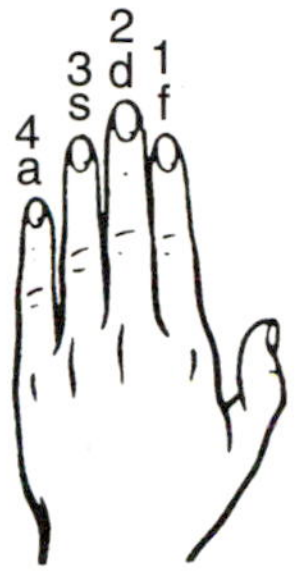

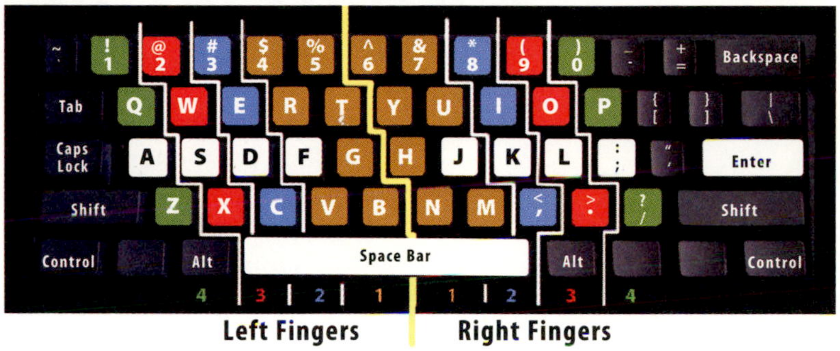

Tap Space Bar once.

1 fff jjj fjf fff jjj fjf fjf jfj jfj fjf
2 ddd kkk dkd ddd kkk dkd dkd kdk kdk dkd

Tap ENTER twice to DS

3 sss lll sls sss lll sls sls lsl lsl sls
4 aaa ;;; a;a aaa ;;; a;s a;a ;a; ;a; a;a

DS

5 ff jj ff jj fj fj fj dd kk dd kk dk dk dk
6 ss ll ss ll sl sl sl aa ;; aa ;; a; a; a;

DS

7 f j d k s l a ;
8 ff jj dd kk ss ll aa ;;
9 fff jjj ddd kkk sss lll aaa jjj ;;;

1d i

1. Apply the standard plan for learning the letter *i*.
2. Key lines 10–12 in the Word Processor. Keep fingers curved. Repeat until you can key it fluently.
3. Click (X) in the upper-right corner of your screen to exit the Word Processor. You will be at the Main menu of *Keyboarding Pro*.

© CENGAGE LEARNING

10 i ik ik ik is is id id if if ill i ail did kid lid
11 i ik aid ail did kid lid lids kids ill aid did ilk
12 id aid aids laid said ids lid skids kiss disk dial

Web-Based Computing: Internet, Cloud, and Web 2.0

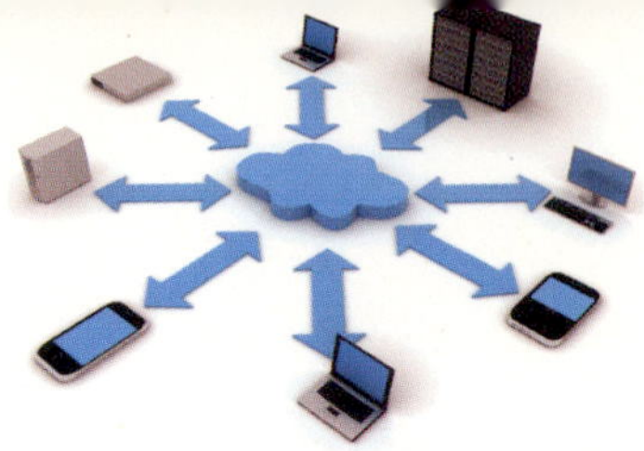

Web-Based Computing 1 | *Internet*

OVERVIEW OF WEB-BASED COMPUTING

Three key components of web-based computing—Internet, Cloud, and Web 2.0—are covered in this section. These topics are overlapping and have many common advantages and disadvantages, but looking at them separately makes it easier to understand the concepts and to apply them in a useful manner.

TIP

Read the *Digital Citizenship* article in *REF2* to learn more about using the Internet effectively and safely.

INTERNET

Most students have had significant experience surfing the Web. If you haven't, a quick terminology review might be helpful.

Internet A global collection of interconnected networks used to share information. To access the Internet, you must have an Internet connection and a browser.

Browser A software program, such as *Internet Explorer*, *Chrome*, and *Firefox* that enables you to view web pages.

URL A **U**niform **R**esource **L**ocater is a unique web address for each web page. Clicking the URL http://www.collegekeyboarding.com will take you to the College Keyboarding website. The protocol is **http://**, the location is **www** (World Wide Web), and the domain is **com** (commercial). Each segment of the address is separated by a period.

Search Engine A software program, such as *Bing*, *Google*, and *Yahoo* that enables you to locate specific information efficiently on the Web by using keywords that describe the topic.

Bookmark A bookmark is a saved URL that you can access quickly by adding it to a **Favorites List**. To visit the website again, click Favorites and select it.

DRILL 1

WEB ACTIVITIES

1. Launch *Internet Explorer* or the browser on your computer.
2. Key the URL http://www.collegekeyboarding.com in the address box at the top of the page. Choose *College Keyboarding 18e*, and then choose *Keyboarding Course Lessons 1-25*. View the information available.
3. Click Favorites on the menu bar and select Add to Favorites. Click the Add button.
4. Click the Back arrow at the top of your browser twice to return to the opening page. Then key weather and click the Search Web button. Check your weather today.

1e Lesson 1 from Software

Read the information at the right. Then do Lesson 1 from *Keyboarding Pro*.

STANDARD PLAN for Using *Keyboarding Pro*

1. Select the Lessons tab. Select a lesson from the drop-down list or key the lesson number (Figure 1-1).
2. The first activity is displayed automatically. Follow the directions on screen. Key from the screen. The software will move automatically to the next activity.

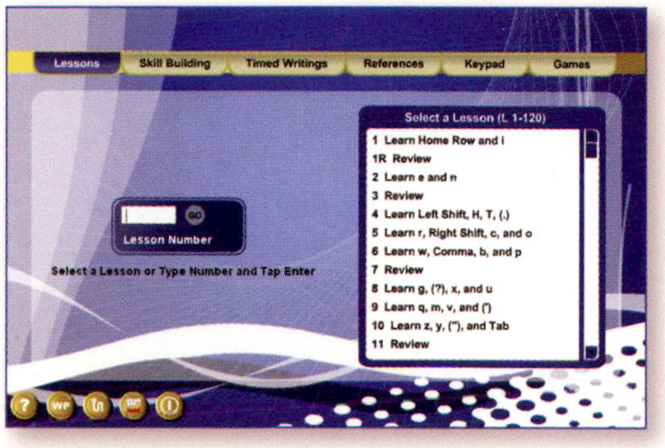

Figure 1-1 Lesson Menu

Figure 1-2 Lesson 1: Learn Home Row and i

3. Key the Textbook Keying activity from the textbook (lines 13–18 below). Click the Stop button to end the activity.
4. Figure 1-3 shows the Lesson Report. A check mark next to the exercise indicates that it is completed.
5. You may print your Lesson Report and view the Performance Graph.
6. From the Main menu, select the Logout button to quit the program. You may choose to transfer your file to another location or send your student record to the Web Reporter.

1f Textbook Keying

1. Key each line once; do not key the numbers. Tap ENTER at the end of each line. Keep your eyes on the book.
2. Click the Stop button to end the activity.

```
13 a  a;  al  ak  aj  s  s;  sl  sk  sj  d  d;  dl  dk  dj
14 j  ja  js  jd  jf  k  ka  ks  kd  kf  l  la  ls  ld  lf
15 a;  sl  a;sl  dkfj  a;sl  dkfj  a;sldkfj  asdf  jk
16 a;  sl  a;sl  dk  fj  dkfj  a;sl  dkfj  fkds;a;  fj
17 f  ff  j  jj  d  dd  k  kk  s  ss  l  ll  a  aa  ;  ;;  fj
18 afj;  a  s  d  f  j  k  l  ;  asdf  jkl;  fdsa  jkl;
```

1g End the Lesson

1. Follow steps 5 and 6 above to print the Lesson Report, send your files to the Web Reporter, and exit the software.
2. Clean up your work area.

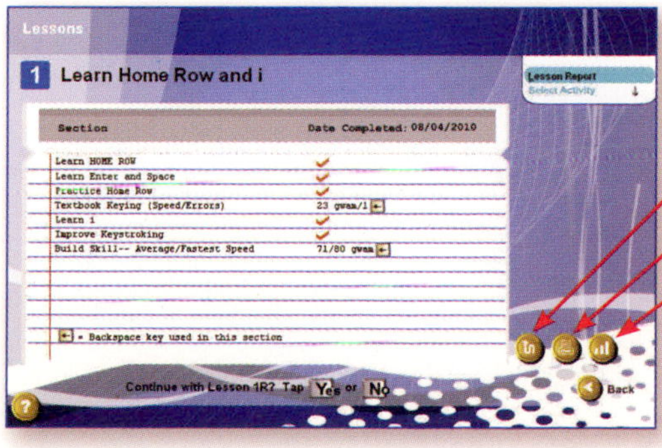

Figure 1-3 Lesson Report Screen

DRILL 22

COMPOSE FOLLOW-UP E-MAIL

1. Compose an e-mail that is a follow-up to the one you prepared in Drill 21. See specific instructions at the right.
2. Edit and proofread your e-mail very carefully.
3. Close and click Next to continue. (*com-drill22*)

Your instructor met with you and gave you many helpful suggestions about preparing for the interview. These suggestions included visiting the recreational center website and learning about the center prior to the interview, tips on dress and conduct during the interview, tips on the kinds of questions that are normally asked during interviews, and overall ways to present yourself more effectively. Your instructor agreed to serve as a reference for you.

Thank your instructor for taking the time to meet with you and indicate how much you appreciate the tips for interviewing that were provided. Be specific enough to show that you listened carefully and learned from the counseling session. Also thank your instructor for being willing to serve as a reference.

DRILL 23

COMPOSE PARAGRAPHS ABOUT CLOUD COMPUTING

1. Read information about the topic cloud computing from a variety of sources. Ideas for locating articles are listed below.
   a. *Web-Based Computing—Cloud Computing* section on pages 100–101.
   b. If you have access to the Internet, key the keyword phrase **cloud computing** and browse for pertinent information.
2. Summarize the information you read about cloud computing in your own words. Compose at least two paragraphs; double-space using the following as a suggested outline.
   a. Explain what cloud computing is and how it is used for communication.
   b. Describe some of the advantages of using cloud computing and some of the disadvantages.
3. Edit and proofread the paragraphs carefully.
4. Close and click Next to continue. (*com-drill23*)

DRILL 24

COMPOSE PARAGRAPHS ABOUT WEB 2.0

1. Read information about Web 2.0 and the variety of Web 2.0 applications available to users today. Ideas for locating articles are listed below.
   a. *Web-Based Computing—Web 2.0* section on page 102.
   b. If you have access to the Internet, browse for pertinent information about Web 2.0 and social media tools. You may prefer to research one of the social media tools referenced in the article on page 102.
2. Summarize the information you read about Web 2.0 and Web 2.0 applications in your own words. Compose at least two paragraphs; double-space using the following as a suggested outline.
   a. Explain what Web 2.0 is and how social media tools are used for communication.
   b. Describe some of the advantages of using social media tools and some of the disadvantages.
3. Edit and proofread the paragraphs carefully.
4. Check and close. (*com-drill24*)

Lesson 1R | *Review*

WARMUP

KEYBOARDING PRO DELUXE 2

Warmup

Getting Started

1. Start *Keyboarding Pro.*
2. Select your name and key your password. Click OK.
3. Select Lesson 1R.
4. Key each exercise as directed in the software.

© CENGAGE LEARNING

Fingers curved and upright

1Ra Textbook Keying

1. Key each line once. Tap ENTER twice to double space (DS) between 2-line groups.
2. Try to keep your eyes on the book the entire time you key.
3. Tap ESC or click Stop to end the exercise.

```
1 f j fjf jj fj fj jf dd kk dd kk dk dk dk
2 s ; s;s ;; s; s; s; aa ;; aa ;; a; a; a;
```

Tap ENTER twice to DS.

```
3 fj dk sl a; fjdksla; jfkdls;a ;a ;s kd j
4 f j fjf d k dkd s l sls a ; fj dk sl a;a
```

DS

```
5 a; al ak aj s s; sl sk sj d d; dl dk djd
6 ja js jd jf k ka ks kd kf l la ls ld lfl
```

Skill Building

1Rb Keyboard Review

Key these lines from the software screen as directed.

```
7 f fa fad s sa sad f fa fall fall l la lad s sa sad
8 a as ask a ad add j ja jak f fa fall; ask; add jak

9 ik ki ki ik is if id il ij ia ij ik is if ji id ia
10 is il ill sill dill fill sid lid ail lid slid jail

11 if is il kid kids ill kid if kids; if a kid is ill
12 is id if ai aid jaks lid sid sis did ail; if lids;

13 a lass; ask dad; lads ask dad; a fall; fall salads
14 as a fad; ask a lad; a lass; all add; a kid; skids

15 as asks did disk ail fail sail ails jail sill silk
16 ask dad; dads said; is disk; kiss a lad; salad lid

17 aid a lad; if a kid is; a salad lid; kiss sad dads
18 as ad all ask jak lad fad kids ill kill fall disks
```

1Rc End the Lesson

1. From the Main Menu, click the Logout button.
2. If instructed, click Yes to send your record to the Web Reporter.
3. If necessary, click Yes to transfer your student record to another location.
4. Exit the software; clean up your work area.

DRILL 20

COMPOSE PARAGRAPHS

1. Write a paragraph of three to five sentences about each of the five topics.
2. Edit and proofread each paragraph carefully.
3. Close and click Next to continue. (*com-drill20*)

1. Write a paragraph introducing yourself to your instructor. Describe the things you think are important in helping her or him get to know you better.
2. Write a paragraph describing one or more of your hobbies.
3. A relative gave you $500 today and suggested that you use it wisely. Write a paragraph discussing what you would do with the money and why you made that decision.
4. You have decided to become more physically fit. Therefore, you plan to improve your eating habits and become more physically active. Write a paragraph describing how you plan to achieve your goal.
5. Two summer jobs are available at a local recreational center. One job is for an assistant in the administrative office; the other is for an assistant to the recreation director.

   The job in the administrative office is varied and includes answering the telephone, scheduling appointments, working with visitors who come to the office, keeping basic records, and doing general office work.

   The job working with the recreation director is an outdoor job that involves coordinating activities for children in various sports, helping to teach children the sports and how to play together, and helping to maintain the various venues.

   Write a paragraph describing the job you would prefer and why you made that selection. Explain how you would be good for the job and how it would be good for you.

DRILL 21

COMPOSE AN E-MAIL

1. Compose an e-mail to your instructor following the instructions.
2. Edit and proofread your e-mail very carefully.
3. Close and click Next to continue. (*com-drill21*)

Describe the job that you selected in Drill 20 and why you chose it. Ask your instructor about the possibility of meeting with you at his or her convenience to help you prepare for your interview. Also ask if you may use her or his name as a reference.

Lesson 2 | *E and N*

WARMUP

KEYBOARDING PRO DELUXE 2 — *Lessons/2a Warmup*

1. Open *Keyboarding Pro.*
2. Locate your student record.
3. Select Lesson 2.

```
1 ff dd ss aa ff dd ss aa jj kk ll ;; fj dk sl a; a;
2 fj dk sl a; fjdksla; a;sldkfj fj dk sl a; fjdksla;

3 aa ss dd ff jj kk ll ;; aa ss dd ff jj kk ll ;; a;
4 if a; as is; kids did; ask a sad lad; if a lass is
```

New Keys

2b E and N

Key each line once; DS between groups.

© CENGAGE LEARNING

e Reach *up* with *left second* finger.

© CENGAGE LEARNING

n Reach *down* with *right first* finger.

e

```
5 e ed ed led led lea lea ale ale elf elf eke eke ed
6 e el el eel els elk elk lea leak ale kale led jell
7 e ale kale lea leak fee feel lea lead elf self eke
```

n

```
8 n nj nj an an and and fan fan and kin din fin land
9 n an fan in fin and land sand din fans sank an sin
10 n in ink sink inn kin skin an and land in din dink
```

all reaches learned

```
11 den end fen ken dean dens ales fend fens keen knee
12 if in need; feel ill; as an end; a lad and a lass;
13 and sand; a keen idea; as a sail sank; is in jail;
14 an idea; an end; a lake; a nail; a jade; a dean is
```

2c Textbook Keying

Key each line once; DS between groups.

TECHNIQUE TIP

Keep your eyes on the textbook copy.

Reach with little finger; tap Enter key quickly; return finger to home key.

```
15 if a lad;
16 is a sad fall
            Tap ENTER twice to DS
17 if a lass did ask
18 ask a lass; ask a lad
                         DS
19 a;sldkfj a;sldkfj a;sldkfj
20 a; sl dk fj fj dk sl a; a;sldkfj
                                DS
21 i ik ik if if is is kid skid did lid aid laid said
22 ik kid ail die fie did lie ill ilk silk skill skid
```

Composition

KEYBOARDING PRO

TIP

Editing and proofreading usually make the difference between high-quality and mediocre writing.

Most careers require good writing skills. You can learn to be an effective writer with practice. Writing at the keyboard facilitates editing and is easier and more effective than handwriting documents. Editing requires complete focus on each of the following areas:

Content accuracy—Determine what needs to be included in a message and then check to see that necessary information is included and that all information is accurate.

Organization—Check sentence structure to see that ideas are presented logically and flow smoothly.

Writing style—Ensure that the message is clear, crisp, concise, and written at an appropriate level.

Mechanical correctness—Check for errors in grammar, spelling, punctuation, capitalization, number usage, and word usage.

COMPOSITION GUIDES

1. Begin with short, easy sentences and paragraphs on topics in which you have knowledge. Then work on putting the sentences and paragraphs together for complete messages.
2. Key your thoughts first and then edit them carefully. It is very difficult to write perfect copy when you begin keying.
3. Use familiar words and a simple, straightforward writing style.
4. Edit to ensure that sentences are carefully arranged, clear, and grammatically correct.
5. Structure paragraphs carefully, making sure that all sentences in the paragraphs relate to the same topic and that they flow logically.
6. Edit and proofread carefully.

DRILL 19

COMPOSE SENTENCES

1. Write and edit one to three complete sentences to answer the five questions.
2. Single-space the response to each question and double-space between questions. Try to use an active, direct style of writing when possible.
3. Close and click Next to continue. (*com-drill19*)

Example

Passive: I find baseball to be enjoyable, and I played well enough to be given the opportunity to play on the team.

Active: I enjoy playing baseball and earned a spot on the team.

1. Where do you live (street name, city or town, and state), and what do you like most and least about the place where you live?
2. Where do you attend school, and what do you like most and least about it?
3. What is your favorite subject, and why do you like it?
4. What is your least favorite subject, and why is it the least favorite?
5. How do you generally spend your time that is not spent in school or sleeping?

Skill Building

2d Reinforcement

Key each line once; concentrate on what you are keying.

23 ik ik ik if is il ik id is if kid did lid aid ails

24 did lid aid; add a line; aid kids; ill kids; id is

n

25 nj nj nj an an and and end den ken in ink sin skin

26 jn din sand land nail sank and dank skin sans sink

e

27 el els elf elk lea lead fee feel sea seal ell jell

28 el eke ale jak lake elf els jaks kale eke els lake

all reaches

29 dine in an inn; fake jade; lend fans; as sand sank

30 in nine inns; if an end; need an idea; seek a fee;

31 if a lad; a jail; is silk; is ill; a dais; did aid

32 adds a line; and safe; asks a lass; sail in a lake

2e End the Lesson

1. If appropriate, send your student record to the Web Reporter.
2. Exit the software; clean up your work area.

WORKPLACE SUCCESS

© ULTRA.F/JUPITERIMAGES

Keyboarding: The Survival Skill

Keyboarding is a valuable and necessary skill for everyone in this technological world. It is an expected tool for effective communication throughout one's life.

Students who resort to "hunting and pecking" to key their school assignments are constantly searching for the correct letter on the keyboard. Frustration abounds for students who wish to key their research report into the computer, but do not have the touch keyboarding skills required to accomplish the task quickly and proficiently. Students who can key by touch are much more relaxed because they can keep their eyes on the screen and concentrate on text editing and composing.

Some people claim that voice-activated computers will replace the need for keyboarding. Voice activation currently works best in conjunction with keyboarding. The first draft of a document can be inputted using voice; the draft is then edited using the keyboard. Together, this process can greatly speed work performance.

DRILL 17

PROOFREADING

1. Key the paragraph, correcting errors as you key. *Hint:* Ten errors are planted in the paragraph.
2. Follow the proofreading and editing procedures in the previous drill.
3. Check and click Next to continue. (*com-drill17*)

The 1st quarter revenue figures for region IV was released today and you will be pleased to learn that once again the team exceded it's first quarter revenue budget. Congradulations! All member of the team exceeded their budget for the first quarter. We have consistently met both team goals for the passed 3 years; but rarely has every member of the team exceeded the budget plan.

DRILL 18

PROOFREADING

1. Key the document double-spaced, correcting errors as you key. *Hint:* Ten errors are planted in the two paragraphs.
2. Follow the proofreading and editing procedures in the previous drill.
3. Check and click Next to continue. (*com-drill18*)

E-mail, once considered to be the most frequently used an misused means of communication is being surpassed by instant messaging and social networking applications, such as Facebook, MySpace, and Twitter. Blogs and wikis also accounts for many messages send in intoday's Web 2.0 society.

Taking advantage of these highly collaborative and targeted means of communication, businesses are creating their own social networking and micro-blogging sites. How ever, business executives share the following concerns: some lack of security for company information, the ease with which messages can be received by unintended recepients, communications being to causal, poor quality of messages, and inappropriateness of the medium for certain types of messages. To be a successful business communicator each employe must understand company communication policy and adhere to the established procedures and practices.

Lesson 3 | *Review*

WARMUP

KEYBOARDING PRO DELUXE 2

Lessons/3a Warmup

Key each line at a steady pace; tap and release each key quickly. Key each line again at a faster pace.

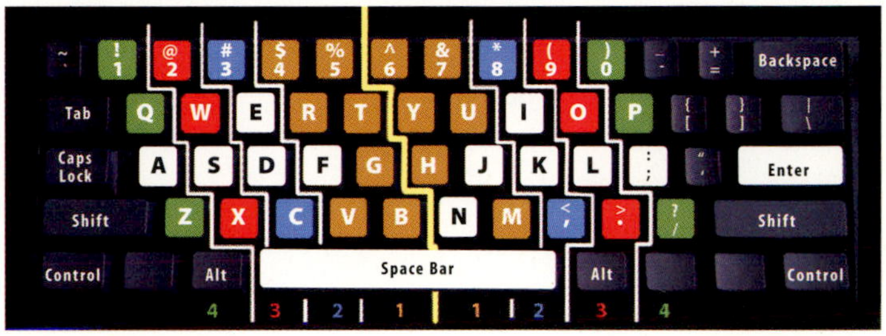


```
home  1 ad ads lad fad dad as ask fa la lass jak jaks alas
   n  2 an fan and land fan flan sans sand sank flank dank
   i  3 is id ill dill if aid ail fail did kid ski lid ilk
 all  4 ade alas nine else fife ken; jell ink jak inns if;
```

Skill Building

3b Textbook Keying

Key each line once. DS between groups.

Lines 5–8: Think and key words. Make the space part of the word.

Lines 9–12: Think and key phrases. Do not key the vertical rules separating the phrases.

easy words

```
 5 if is as an ad el and did die eel fin fan elf lens
 6 as ask and id kid and ade aid eel feel ilk skis an
 7 ail fail aid did ken ale led an flan inn inns alas
 8 eel eke nee kneel did kids kale sees lake elf fled
```

easy phrases — **Tap ENTER twice**

```
 9 el  el|id  id|is  is|eke  eke|lee  lee|ale  ale|jill  jak
10 is  if|is  a|is  a|a  disk|a  disk|did  ski|did  ski|is  a
11 sell  a|sell  a|sell  a  sled|fall  fad|fall  fad|fad  is
12 sees  a  lake|sees  a  lake|as  a  deal|sell  sled|a  sale
```

3c Technique Practice

Key each line once.

TECHNIQUE TIP

Reach with the little finger; tap Enter key quickly; return finger to home key.

home row: fingers curved and upright

```
13 jak lad as lass dad sad lads fad fall la ask ad as
14 asks add jaks dads a lass ads flak adds sad as lad
```

upward reaches: straighten fingers slightly; return quickly to home position

```
15 fed die led ail kea lei did ale fife silk leak lie
16 sea lid deal sine desk lie ale like life idea jail
```

double letters: don't hurry when stroking double letters

```
17 fee jell less add inn seek fall alee lass keel all
18 dill dell see fell eel less all add kiss seen sell
```

DRILL 15

PROOFREADING

1. Key the paragraph, correcting errors as you key. *Hint:* Ten errors are planted in the paragraph.
2. Follow the proofreading and editing procedures in the previous drill.
3. Check and click Next to continue. (*com-drill15*)

Blogs are Web logs (personnel journals) that is typically owned and maintained by 1 person. A blog gives it's owner a place to write about any topic of interest. It is typical updated frequently, much as a travelog or dairy would be. Only the owner can edit, delete, or add to the content of a blog. Visitors can comment about the content but they cannot change if. Wikis differ from blogs in this respect, since any body can change anything in a wiki.

DRILL 16

PROOFREADING

1. Proofread each sentence and then key the sentence correcting the error in it. Use the Numbering command to number each item.
2. Proofread again to ensure that you did not make any other keying errors. Correct any errors you find.
3. Check and click Next to continue. (*com-drill16*)

1. The only way to proofread numbers effectively is too compare the keyed copy to the original source.
2. Concentration is an important proofreading skill, especially it you proofread on screen.
3. May people skip over the small words when they proofread; yet the small words often contain errors.
4. They sole 15 baskets at $30 each for a total of $450. Always check the math when you proofread.
5. Names are often spelled in different ways; there fore, you must verify the spelling to ensure that you use the correct version.
6. Reading copy on a word-bye-word basis is necessary to locate all errors.
7. Checking for words that my have been left out is also important.
8. Of course, you should also check to make sure the content in correct.

3d Rhythm Builder

Think and key phrases. Do not key the vertical rules separating the phrases.

phrases (think and key phrases)

19 and and land land el el elf elf self self ail nail
20 as as ask ask ad ad lad lad id id lid lid kid kids

21 if if | is is | jak jak | all all | did did | nan nan | elf elf
22 as a lad | ask dad | fed a jak | as all ask | sales fad

23 sell a lead | seal a deal | feel a leaf | if a jade sale
24 is a | is as if | a disk | aid all kids | did ski | is a silk

3e Textbook Keying

Key each line once; DS between 2-line groups.

© CENGAGE LEARNING

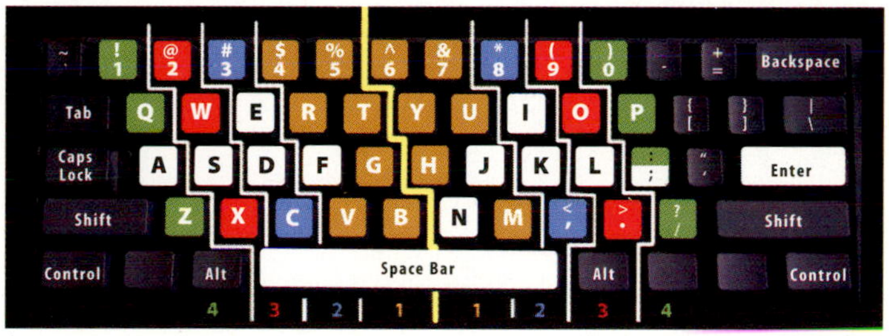

TECHNIQUE TIP

Tap keys quickly.
Tap the Space Bar with down-and-in motion.
Tap Enter with a quick flick of the little finger.

reach review

25 ea sea lea seas deal leaf leak lead leas flea keas
26 as ask lass ease as asks ask ask sass as alas seas
DS
27 sa sad sane sake sail sale sans safe sad said sand
28 le sled lead flee fled ale flea lei dale kale leaf
DS
29 jn jn nj nj in fan fin an; din ink sin and inn an;
30 de den end fen an an and and ken knee nee dean dee

3f Timed Writing

1. Key lines 35–38 for 1'. If you finish before time is up, repeat the lines.
2. Practice the remaining lines in the game.
3. End your lesson.
4. Clean up your work area.

d/e
31 den end fen ken dean dens ales fend fens keen knee
32 a deed; a desk; a jade; an eel; a jade eel; a dean

n/a
33 an an in in and and en end end sane sane sand sand
34 a land; a dean; a fan; a fin; a sane end; end land

e/n
35 el eel eld elf sell self el dell fell elk els jell
36 in fin inn inks dine sink fine fins kind line lain

all reaches
37 an and fan dean elan flan land lane lean sand sane
38 sell a lead; sell a jade; seal a deal; feel a leaf

DRILL 13

PROOFREADING

1. Key the paragraph, correcting errors as you key. *Hint:* Ten errors are planted in the paragraph.
2. Proofread the copy carefully on the screen. Make needed corrections. Preview the document and print it.
3. Proofread the hard copy carefully and mark any uncorrected errors, using proofreaders' marks.
4. Make the corrections in the document file.
5. Check and click Next to continue. (*com-drill13*)

The executive committee plans to meet on April second at one o'clock in room 201 to develop a strategic plan to market our new products At it's last monthly meeting David Westfield, a leading Consultant with the Jones Group presented several alternatives. Mr Westfield will present a proposal at this meeting for consulting services from the Jones Group to assist us in planning the new product launch.

DRILL 14

PROOFREADING

1. Key the paragraph, correcting errors as you key. Hint: Ten errors are planted in the paragraph.
2. Follow the proofreading and editing procedures in the previous drill.
3. Check and click Next to continue. (*com-drill14*)

Editing and proof-reading is just as important for internal documents as for external documents. However, many people wrong beleive that external documents need carefully scrutiny but documents that stay with in the company do not matter as much. If your e-mails are memos frequently contain errors, fellow workers and supervisors may think that you are careless or have poor communication skills. This perception may harm your chances for advancement within you company. Developing good communication skills, and applying those skills to each document that you produce will enhance your career opportunities.

Lesson 4 | *Left Shift, H, T, Period*

WARMUP

KEYBOARDING PRO DELUXE 2

Lessons/4a Warmup

Key each line twice. Keep eyes on copy.

home row	1	`al as ads lad dad fad jak fall lass asks fads all;`
e/i/n	2	`ed ik jn in knee end nine line sine lien dies leis`
all reaches	3	`see a ski; add ink; fed a jak; is an inn; as a lad`
easy	4	`an dial id is an la lake did el ale fake is land a`

New Keys

4b Left Shift and h

Key each line once.

Follow the "Standard Procedures for Learning New Keyreaches" on p. 4 for all remaining reaches.

left shift Reach *down* with *left fourth* (little) finger; shift, tap, release.

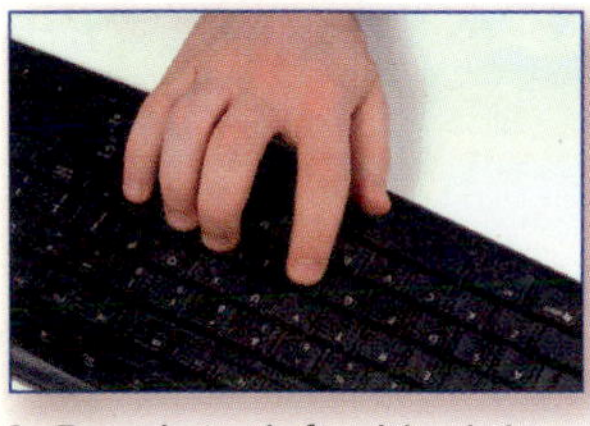

h Reach to *left* with *right first* finger.

left shift

```
5  J Ja Ja Jan Jan Jane Jana Ken Kass Lee Len Nan Ned
6  and Ken and Lena and Jake and Lida and Nan and Ida
7  Inn is; Jill Ina is; Nels is; Jen is; Ken Lin is a
```

Hal has hands

h

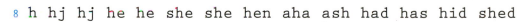

```
8  h hj hj he he she she hen aha ash had has hid shed
9  h hj ha hie his half hand hike dash head sash shad
10 aha hi hash heal hill hind lash hash hake dish ash
```

all reaches learned

```
11 Nels Kane and Jake Jenn; she asked Hi and Ina Linn
12 Lend Lana and Jed a dish; I fed Lane and Jess Kane
13 I see Jake Kish and Lash Hess; Isla and Helen hike
```

4c Textbook Keying

Key the drill once: Strive for good control.

```
14 he she held a lead; she sells jade; she has a sale
15 Ha Ja Ka La Ha Hal Ja Jake Ka Kahn La Ladd Ha Hall
16 Hal leads; Jeff led all fall; Hal has a safe lead
17 Hal Hall heads all sales; Jake Hess asks less fee;
```

Proofreaders' Marks

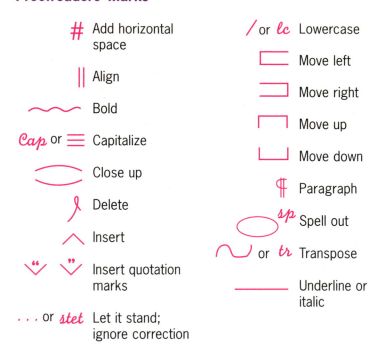

- # Add horizontal space
- || Align
- ~~~ Bold
- *Cap* or ≡ Capitalize
- Close up
- Delete
- ^ Insert
- Insert quotation marks
- . . . or *stet* Let it stand; ignore correction
- / or *lc* Lowercase
- Move left
- Move right
- Move up
- Move down
- ¶ Paragraph
- *sp* Spell out
- or *tr* Transpose
- Underline or italic

DRILL 12

PROOFREADERS' MARKS

1. Key the paragraph, correcting errors as you key. Refer to the proofreaders' mark at the top of the page.
2. Proofread the copy carefully on the screen following the guides on the previous page. Make appropriate corrections including your keying errors.
3. Preview the document and print it.
4. Proofread the hard copy carefully and mark any uncorrected errors using proofreaders' marks. Make the corrections in the document file.
5. Check and click Next to continue. (*com-drill12*)

Instant messaging began as a popular tool for determining if friends were on line and were willing to play games or chat. Now its moving to the corporatesetting. The number of instant messages send at work increased 110% last year. with IM, messages fly back and forth, faster then e-mail. Workers use IM to get urgently needed information, send important news signal that a client is waiting, and avoid telephone tag. 2 problems with instant messaging have been lack of security an the inability to keep a record of Correspondence. New business versions of Im software are addressing this issues.

4d t and . (period)

Key each line once.

Period: Space once after a period that follows an initial or an abbreviation. To increase readability, space twice after a period that ends a sentence.

Hal hit this.##

t Reach *up* with *left first* finger.

. (period) Reach *down* with *right third* finger.

t

18 t tf tf aft aft left fit fat fete tiff tie the tin

19 tf at at aft lit hit tide tilt tint sits skit this

20 hat kit let lit ate sit flat tilt thin tale tan at

Ted hit this. ##

. (period)

21 .l .l l.l fl. fl. L. L. Neal and J. N. List hiked.

22 Hand J. H. Kass a fan. Jess did. I need an idea.

23 Jane said she has a tan dish; Jae and Lee need it.

all reaches learned

24 I did tell J. K. that Lt. Li had left. He is ill.

25 tie tan kit sit fit hit hat; the jet left at nine.

26 I see Lila and Ilene at tea. Jan Kane ate at ten.

Skill Building

4e Reinforcement

Key with control; concentrate as you practice the new reaches.

reach review

27 tf .l hj ft ki de jh tf ik ed hj de ft ki l. tf ik

28 elf eel left is sis fit till dens ink has delt ink

h/e

29 he he heed heed she she shelf shelf shed shed she

30 he has; he had; he led; he sleds; she fell; he is

i/t

31 it is if id did lit tide tide tile tile list list

32 it is; he hit it; he is ill; she is still; she is

shift

33 Hal and Nel; Jade dishes; Kale has half; Jed hides

34 Hi Ken; Helen and Jen hike; Jan has a jade; Ken is

enter

35 Nan had a sale.

36 He did see Hal.

37 Lee has a desk.

38 Ina hid a dish.

TECHNIQUE TIP

Tap Enter without pausing or looking up from the copy.

Proofreading

KEYBOARDING PRO

References/Communication Skills/Proofreading

TIP

Learn to proofread on the screen first and then as a last check, proofread the printed document again.

Often the difference between high-quality and mediocre documents is in how carefully they are proofread. Careful proofreading ensures the accuracy of the final document.

Proofreading requires complete focus on each of the following areas:

Overall appearance of a document—check for appropriate stationery, attractive placement, and correct and consistent format.

Content accuracy—check for accuracy and completeness, such as making sure dates are correct and times are not left off.

Mechanical correctness—check for keying errors, as well as mistakes in spelling, grammar, punctuation, capitalization, word usage, and number usage. Review basic guides if you are not comfortable with your knowledge level in each of the areas listed.

PROOFREADING GUIDES

1. Check the document using the Spelling and Grammar commands.
2. Proofread the document on the screen slowly, on a word-by-word basis. Focus on words that may be spelled correctly but are misused, such as *you/your, is/in, if/it, there/their, two/to/too, then/than,* and *principle/principal.*
3. Check specifically for capitalization, punctuation, and number usage.
4. Check to see that the document is complete, ensuring that enclosure or copy notations are not left off.
5. Verify that each number is correct. The only way to ensure that a number is correct is to check it against the source from which it was keyed.
6. Preview the document on screen to ensure that placement is appropriate.
7. Print the document and proofread it again. It is helpful to use a guide (ruler, large envelope, or folded sheet of paper). Move it down line by line as you read. Mark the corrections using proofreaders' marks. Refer to a list of common proofreaders' marks found on the next page.

TIP

An error in a number could have significant negative consequences; for example, keying $300,000 rather than $400,000 in quoting a price or authorizing a loan at 7% when the correct percentage is 8% could prove to be very costly.

PROOFREADING STATISTICAL COPY

Statistical copy requires special attention. It is very easy to make errors in keying numbers, and it is very difficult to determine if a number keyed is correct. The same thing is true for a date or time.

1. Verify numbers against the original source; verify dates against the calendar; and check computations with a calculator.
2. Read numbers in groups. For example, the telephone number 618-555-0123 can be read in three parts: *six-one-eight, five-five-five, zero-one-two-three.*
3. Read numbers aloud and preferably with a partner checking against the original copy.

WARMUP

KEYBOARDING PRO DELUXE 2 — *Lessons/5a Warmup*

Key each line twice.

home keys 1 a; ad add al all lad fad jak ask lass fall jak lad

t/h/i/n 2 the hit tin nit then this kith dint tine hint thin

left shift/. 3 I need ink. Li has an idea. Hit it. I see Kate.

all reaches 4 Jeff ate at ten; he left a salad dish in the sink.

New Keys

5b r and Right Shift

Key each line once.

© CENGAGE LEARNING

r Reach *up* with *left first* finger.

© CENGAGE LEARNING

right shift Reach *down* with *right fourth* finger; shift, tap, release.

r

5 r rf rf riff riff fir fir rid ire jar air sir lair

6 rf rid ark ran rat are hare art rant tire dirt jar

7 rare dirk ajar lark rain kirk share hart rail tart

right shift

8 D D Dan Dan Dale Ti Sal Ted Ann Ed Alf Ada Sid Fan

9 and Sid and Dina and Allen and Eli and Dean and Ed

10 Ed Dana; Dee Falk; Tina Finn; Sal Alan; Anna Deeds

all reaches learned

11 Jane and Ann hiked in the sand; Asa set the tents.

12 a rake; a jar; a tree; a red fire; a fare; a rain;

13 Fred Derr and Rai Tira dined at the Tree Art Fair.

5c Textbook Keying

Key each line once; DS between 2-line groups.

14 ir ir ire fir first air fair fire tire rid sir

15 fir jar tar fir flit rill till list stir dirt fire

DS

16 Feral is ill. Dan reads. Dee and Ed Finn see Dere.

17 All is still as Sarah and I fish here in the rain.

DS

18 I still see a red ash tree that fell in the field.

19 Lana said she did sail her skiff in the dark lake.

Spelling

KEYBOARDING PRO

References/Communication Skills/Spelling

DRILL 10

SPELLING

1. Proofread the sentences. If the word shown in bold is spelled correctly, key **Yes**. If the work is misspelled, key **No**.
2. Check and click Next to continue. (*com-drill10*)

1. The sign in the store window stated that **turkeyes** are in the meat department.
2. Only cash or **checkes** are accepted in the new ice cream shop.
3. The postal clerk checked the **weight** of the package.
4. Students with fewer than three absences **recieved** special recognition.
5. Two **keys** were issued to each residence hall student.
6. How can celebrity chefs measure **accurately** without using a measuring spoon?
7. The complimentary closing very **truley** yours is seldom used in business correspondence.
8. You will find a list of school **supplies** in a display at the front of the store.
9. Be sure you have **submited** your travel budget request by the first of the year.
10. My parents traveled to Vermont for the turning of the **leaves**.

DRILL 11

COMPREHENSIVE REVIEW

1. Key the paragraph, correcting errors as you key. The ten errors include capitalization, number expression, subject-verb agreement, pronoun case and agreement, commas, and spelling errors.
2. Check and click Next to continue. (*com-drill11*)

Scheduled for Monday june 15 at one p.m. in room two this week's orientation training session focuses on netiquette. in preparation for this meeting each participant are asked to bring thier three pet peeves regarding misuse of email instant messaging and discussion forumes. prizes will be awarded to the first 5 individuals whom register.

5d c and o

Key each line once.

c Reach *down* with *left second* finger.

o Reach *up* with *right third* finger.

Rick can kick.

c

20 c c cd cd cad cad can can tic ice sac cake cat sic
21 clad chic cite cheek clef sick lick kick dice rice
22 call acid hack jack lack lick cask crack clan cane

Otto sold lotto.

o

23 o ol ol old old of off odd ode or ore oar soar one
24 ol sol sold told dole do doe lo doll sol solo odor
25 onto door toil lotto soak fort hods foal roan load

all reaches learned

26 Carlo Rand can call Rocco; Cole can call Doc Cost.
27 Trina can ask Dina if Nick Corl has left; Joe did.
28 Case sent Carole a nice skirt; it fits Lorna Rich.

Skill Building

5e Keyboard Reinforcement

Key each line once; key at a steady pace. Strive for control.

TECHNIQUE TIP

Reach up without moving hands away from your body. Use quick keystrokes.

o/r
29 or or for for nor nor ore ore oar oar roe roe sore
30 a rose | her or | he or | he rode | or for | a door | her doll

i/t
31 is is tis tis it it fit fit tie tie this this lits
32 it is | it is | it is this | it is this | it sits | tie fits

e/n
33 en en end end ne ne need need ken ken kneel kneels
34 lend the | lend the | at the end | at the end | need their

c/o
35 ch ch check check ck ck hack lack jack co co cones
36 the cot | the cot | a dock | a dock | a jack | a jack | a cone

all reaches
37 Jack and Rona did frost nine of the cakes at last.
38 Jo can ice her drink if Tess can find her a flask.
39 Ask Jean to call Fisk at noon; he needs her notes.

Subject-Verb Agreement

KEYBOARDING PRO

References/Communication Skills/ Subject-Verb Agreement

DRILL 8

SUBJECT-VERB AGREEMENT

1. Key the sentences, choosing the correct verb. Use the Numbering command to number each item.
2. Proofread, check, and click Next to continue. (*com-drill8*)

1. Everything in the packages (is/are) securely wrapped.
2. None of the mountains (is/are) visible today.
3. Many of the drivers (is/are) following too closely.
4. Everyone (is/are) expected to attend the seminar.
5. All of the candidates (was/were) invited to the debate.
6. Nobody (want/wants) to be left behind.
7. Few of the animals (is/are) outside today.

DRILL 9

SUBJECT-VERB AGREEMENT

1. Key the sentences, choosing the correct verb and applying the correct commas and capitalization. Use the Numbering command to number each item.
2. Proofread, check, and click Next to continue. (*com-drill9*)

1. both of the curies (was/were) nobel prize winners.
2. mr. and mrs. thomas funderburk, jr. (was/were) married on Saturday november 23 1936 and they established their first home in Seattle Washington.
3. my sister and her college roommates (plan/plans) to tour london paris and rome this summer.
4. Emma Greer our new information manager (suggest/suggests) the following salutation when using an attention line: ladies and gentlemen.
5. the body language expert (place/places) his hand on his cheek as he says "touch your hand to your chin."
6. the japanese child (enjoy/enjoys) the american food her hosts (serve/serves) her.
7. the final exam (cover/covers) chapters 1-5.
8. Each of the directors in the sales department (has/have) given (his or her, their) approval.
9. According to bylaw 5-21 all of the candidates (are/is) invited to the debate at boston college.

Lesson 6 | *W, Comma, B, P*

WARMUP

KEYBOARDING PRO DELUXE 2

Lessons/6a Warmup

Key each line twice; avoid pauses.

home row 1 ask a lad; a fall fad; had a salad; ask a sad jak;

o/t 2 to do it; to toil; as a tot; do a lot; he told her

c/r 3 cots are; has rocks; roll cot; is rich; has an arc

all reaches 4 Holt can see Dane at ten; Jill sees Frank at nine.

New Keys

6b **w** and **,** (comma)

Key each line once.

Comma: Space once after a comma.

win, won, now

Will will own a cow, owl, wolf.

© CENGAGE LEARNING

w Reach *up* with *left third* finger.

© CENGAGE LEARNING

, (comma) Reach *down* with *right second* finger.

w

5 w ws ws was was wan wit low win jaw wilt wink wolf

6 sw sw ws ow ow now now row row own own wow wow owe

7 to sew; to own; was rich; was in; is how; will now

, (comma)

8 k, k, k, irk, ilk, ask, oak, ark, lark, jak, rock,

9 skis, a dock, a fork, a lock, a fee, a tie, a fan,

10 Jo, Ed, Ted, and Dan saw Nan in a car lift; a kit

all reaches learned

11 Win, Lew, Drew, and Walt will walk to West Willow.

12 Ask Ho, Al, and Jared to read the code; it is new.

13 The window, we think, was closed; we felt no wind.

6c Textbook Keying

Key each line once.

14 walk wide sown wild town went jowl wait white down

15 a dock, a kit, a wick, a lock, a row, a cow, a fee

16 Joe lost to Ron; Fiji lost to Cara; Don lost to Al

17 Kane will win; Nan will win; Rio will win; Di wins

18 Walter is in Reno; Tia is in Tahoe; then to Hawaii

Pronoun Agreement

KEYBOARDING PRO

References/Communication Skills/Pronoun Agreement

DRILL 6

PRONOUN AGREEMENT

1. For each sentence, select the correct pronoun from the two choices shown in parentheses.
2. Key just the correct pronoun for each sentence. Use the Numbering command to number each item.
3. Check and click Next to continue. (*com-drill6*)

1. Each student must have (his or her, their) own data disk.
2. Several students have (his or her, their) own computer.
3. All candidates must submit (his or her, their) resume.
4. Napoleon organized (his, their) armies.
5. The company presented (its, their) five-year plan.
6. Jane and Alfredo sent (his and her, their) contribution.
7. Neither Chris nor Joseph wants to do (his, their) share.
8. Someone was talking on (his or her, their) cell phone and not watching the road.
9. Everybody should find a technique for stress management that works well for (him or her, them).

Commas

KEYBOARDING PRO

References/Communication Skills/Commas

DRILL 7

COMMAS

1. Key the sentences, correcting the commas. Use the Numbering command to number each item.
2. Proofread, check, and click Next to continue. (*com-drill7*)

1. The legislators voted on Policy #2083 on May 23 2011 at 5 p.m.
2. To view Michelle's entire social networking site I need her permission.
3. The parents volunteered to bring coffee juice milk and pastries.
4. Several club members designed an attractive logo and the fundraising committee created an online store for selling merchandise displaying the logo.
5. Mr. Rankin explained "Upload your essay to the class blog by Monday at 9 a.m."
6. The independent film festival will be held in Baton Rouge Louisiana on May 11-15.
7. Chef Nate I appreciate your answering my questions about organic gardening on your blog.

6d b and p

Key each line once.

b Reach *down* with *left first* finger.

p Reach *up* with *right fourth* (little) finger.

Bob wants pop.

b

19 bf bf bf biff fib fib bib bib boa boa fib fibs rob
20 bf bf bf ban ban bon bon bow bow be be rib rib sob
21 a dob, a cob, a crib, a lab, a slab, a bid, a bath

p

22 p; p; pa pa; pal pal pan pan pad par pen pep paper
23 pa pa; lap lap; nap nap; hep ape spa asp leap clap
24 a park, a pan, a pal, a pad, apt to pop, a pair of

all reaches learned

25 Barb and Bob wrapped a pepper in paper and ribbon.
26 Rip, Joann, and Dick were all closer to the flash.
27 Bo will be pleased to see Japan; he works in Oslo.

Skill Building

6e Keyboard Reinforcement

Key each line once; key at a steady pace.

reach review

28 ki kid did aid lie hj has has had sw saw wits will
29 de dell led sled jn an en end ant hand k, end, kin

s/w

30 ws ws lows now we shown win cow wow wire jowl when
31 Wes saw an owl in the willow tree in the old lane.

b/p

32 bf bf fib rob bid ;p p; pal pen pot nap hop cap bp
33 Rob has both pans in a bin at the back of the pen.

6f Speed Builder

Key each line twice. Work for fluency.

34 to do | can do | to bow | ask her | to nap | to work | is born
35 for this | if she | is now | did all | to see | or not | or if

all reaches

36 Dick owns a dock at this lake; he paid Ken for it.
37 Jane also kept a pair of owls, a hen, and a snake.

38 Blair soaks a bit of the corn, as he did in Japan.
39 I blend the cocoa in the bowl when I work for Leo.

DRILL 4

COMPOSITION

1. DS the paragraph, inserting a proper noun in each blank and applying correct capitalization and number expression.
2. Proofread, check, and click Next to continue. (*com-drill4*)

last _________, my friend _________ and I had a holiday, so we decided to make the most of our day and take a bicycle trip to _________. before leaving, we stopped at _________ to purchase some high-energy foods to sustain us on our trip. we packed our saddle bags and left about _________ o'clock, traveling _________ on _________ street. although we were not on a sight-seeing trip, we did pass _________and _________. by _________ p.m., we returned home exhausted from our journey of _________ miles.

Pronoun Case

KEYBOARDING PRO

References/Communication Skills/Pronoun Case

DRILL 5

PRONOUN CASE

1. For each sentence, select the correct pronoun from the two choices shown in parentheses.
2. Key just the correct pronoun for each sentence. Use the Numbering command to number each item.
3. Check and click Next to continue. (*com-drill5*)

1. Was it Jane and (her, she) who starred in the movie?
2. The players who were injured were Dominique and (I, me).
3. With (who, whom) will you serve as an intern?
4. Our instructor invited (they, them) to the meeting.
5. (Who, Whom) will referee the game tonight?
6. Pat and (me, I) will be the pet sitters for Andy.
7. The problem with the delivery was between Joe and (they, them).
8. Lea and (he, him) had the highest scores on the test.
9. They bought expensive gifts for JoAnn and (I, me).
10. It was (her, she) who answered the phone.

Lesson 7 | Review

WARMUP

KEYBOARDING PRO DELUXE 2 — *Lessons/7a Warmup*

Key each line twice; begin new lines promptly.

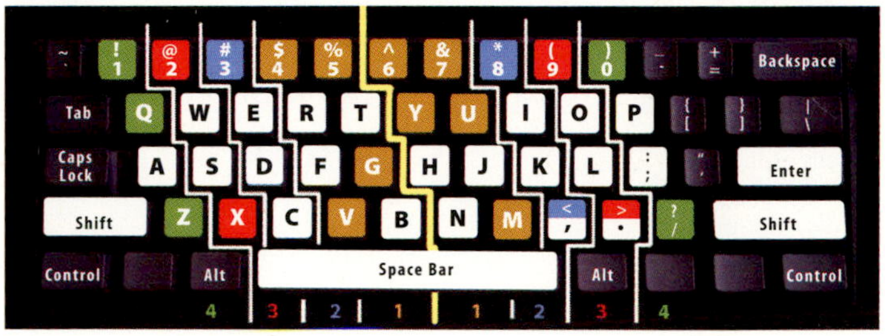

all 1 We often can take the older jet to Paris and back.
home 2 a; sl dk fj a;sl dkfj ad as all ask fads adds asks
1st row 3 Ann Bascan and Cabal Naban nabbed a cab in Canada.
3rd row 4 Rip went to a water show with either Pippa or Pia.

Skill Building

7b Textbook Keying

Key each line once; DS between 3-line groups.

5 ws ws was was wan wan wit wit pew paw nap pop bawl
6 bf bf fb fb fob fob rib rib be be job job bat back
7 p; p; asp asp pan pan ap ap ca cap pa nap pop prow

DS

8 Barb and Bret took an old black robe and the boot.
9 Walt saw a wisp of white water renew ripe peppers.
10 Pat picked a black pepper for the picnic at Parks.

7c Textbook Keying

Key each line once; DS between 3-line groups.

words 11 a an pan so sot la lap ah own do doe el elf to tot
phrases 12 if it | to do | it is | do so | for the | he works | if he bid
sentences 13 Jess ate all of the peas in the salad in the bowl.

DS

words 14 bow bowl pin pint for fork forks hen hens jak jaks
phrases 15 is for | did it | is the | we did a | and so | to see | or not
sentences 16 I hid the ace in a jar as a joke; I do not see it.

DS

words 17 chap chaps flak flake flakes prow prowl work works
phrases 18 as for the | as for the | and to the | to see it | and did
sentences 19 As far as I know, he did not read all of the book.

TECHNIQUE TIP

words: key as a single unit rather than letter by letter;
phrases: say and key fluently;
sentences: work for fluency.

DRILL 2

CAPITALIZATION

1. Key the paragraphs, correcting all errors in capitalization.
2. Proofread, check, and click Next to continue. (*com-drill2*)

as you requested, this past week i visited the facilities of the magnolia conference center in isle of palms, south carolina. bob bremmerton, group manager, was my host for the visit.

magnolia offers many advantages for our johns and lovett Leadership training conference scheduled for june 25-27, 2011. The prices are reasonable; the facilities are excellent; the location is suitable. In addition to the beachfront location, tennis and golf packages are part of the group price.

Number Expression

KEYBOARDING PRO

References/Communication Skills/Number Expression

DRILL 3

NUMBER EXPRESSION

1. Key each sentence, correcting the number expression errors. Use the Numbering command to number each item.
2. Proofread, check, and click Next to continue. (*com-drill3*)

1. Address the letter to 1 Elm Street and postmark by April 15th.
2. The retirement reception will be held on the 1st of May in Room Twelve at 5 o'clock.
3. Program participants included fifteen supervisors, five managers, and two vice presidents.
4. 12 boxes arrived damaged and about 2/3 of the contents were crushed.
5. The manager reported that 85% of the project was complete with 9 days remaining until the March 15th due date.
6. The presiding officer called the meeting to order at two p.m. and requested that the 2 50-page reports be distributed.
7. Nearly 10 million people visited the virtual museum this year.
8. Jim lives at nine 21st Street and works on 6th Avenue.
9. The attorney quoted from Section two of the code.
10. The parents of the Twin Cities Futbol Club have raised about 50 percent of the money for the tournament.

7d Technique Practice

Key each set of lines once.

▼ Space once after a period following an abbreviation.

spacing: space *immediately* after each word

20 ad la as in if it lo no of oh he or so ok pi be we
21 an ace ads ale aha a fit oil a jak nor a bit a pew
22 ice ades born is fake to jail than it and the cows

spacing/shifting

23 Ask Jed. Dr.▼ Han left at ten; Dr.▼ Crowe, at nine.
24 I asked Jin if she had ice in a bowl; it can help.
25 Freda, not Jack, went to Spain. Joan likes Spain.

7e Timed Writing

1. Take two 1' writings. If you finish before time is up, begin again. Do not tap ENTER at the ends of the lines.
2. End the lesson. Go to the Word Processor and complete 7f.

Goal: 12 *gwam.*

	gwam
It is hard to fake a confident spirit. We will do	10
better work if we approach and finish a job and	20
know that we will do the best work we can and then	30
not fret.	32

| 1 | 2 | 3 | 4 | 5 | 6 | 7 | 8 | 9 | 10 |

7f Using the Word Processor Timer

Exercises to be keyed in the Word Processor are identified with the Word Processor icon. Key the timing in 7e. Follow the instructions in the textbook and key from the textbook.

STANDARD PLAN for Using the Word Processor Timer

You can check your speed in the Word Processor using the Timer.

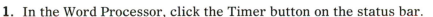

1. In the Word Processor, click the Timer button on the status bar.
2. The Timer begins once you start to key and stops automatically.
3. To save the timing, click the File menu and Save as. Use your initals (*xx*), the exercise number, and number of the timing as the filename. Example: *xx-7f-t1* (your initials, exercise 7f, timing1).
4. Click the Timer button again to start a new timing.
5. Each new timing must be saved with its own name.

7g Word Processor

1. In the Word Processor, key each line once for fluency. Do not save your work.
2. Set the Timer in the Word Processor for 30". Take two 30" writings on each line. Do not save the timings.

Goal: to reach the end of the line before time is up.

	gwam
26 Dan took her to the show.	12
27 Jan lent the bowl to the pros.	14
28 Hold the wrists low for this drill.	16
29 Jessie fit the black panel to the shelf.	18
30 Jake held a bit of cocoa and an apricot for Diane.	20
31 Dick and I fish for cod on the docks at Fish Lake.	20
32 Kent still held the dish and the cork in his hand.	20

| 1 | 2 | 3 | 4 | 5 | 6 | 7 | 8 | 9 | 10 |

Communication Skills

A review and quick check of basic communication skills, including capitalization, number expression, pronouns, commas, subject-verb agreement, spelling, proofreading, and composition, are presented in this section using activities in the *Keyboarding Pro 6* software and drills provided below and on the following pages. To gain maximum benefit from this condensed review, always complete the pretest, review of the rules, and the posttest in *Keyboarding Pro 6* first before completing the textbook drills. Follow the path below each communication skill to locate the appropriate *Keyboarding Pro 6* activities.

Capitalization

KEYBOARDING PRO

References/Communication Skills/Capitalization

DRILL 1

CAPITALIZATION

1. Key the sentences, correcting all capitalization errors. Use the Numbering command to number each item.
2. Proofread again to ensure that you did not make any other keying errors. Correct any errors you find.
3. Check and click Next to continue. (*com-drill1*)

1. according to one study, the largest ethnic minority group online is hispanics.
2. the american author mark twain said, "always do right; this will gratify some people and astonish the rest."
3. the grand canyon was formed by the colorado river cutting into the high-plateau region of northwestern arizona.
4. the president of russia is elected by popular vote.
5. the hubble space telescope is a cooperative project of the european space agency and the national aeronautics and space administration.
6. the train left north station at 6:45 this morning.
7. the trademark cyberprivacy prevention act would make it illegal for individuals to purchase domains solely for resale and profit.
8. consumers spent $7 billion online between november 1 and december 31, 2010, compared to $3.1 billion for the same period in 2009.
9. new students should attend an orientation session on wednesday, august 15, at 8 a.m. in room 252 of the perry building.
10. the summer book list includes *where the red fern grows* and *the mystery of the missing baseball.*

Lesson 8 | G, Question Mark, X, U

WARMUP

KEYBOARDING PRO DELUXE 2 *Lessons/8a Warmup*

Key each line twice. Keep eyes on copy.

all 1 Dick will see Job at nine if Rach sees Pat at one.
w/b 2 As the wind blew, Bob Webber saw the window break.
p/, 3 Pat, Pippa, or Cap has prepared the proper papers.
all 4 Bo, Jose, and Will fed Lin; Jack had not paid her.

New Keys

8b g and ?

Key each line once; repeat.

Question mark: The question mark is usually followed by two spaces.

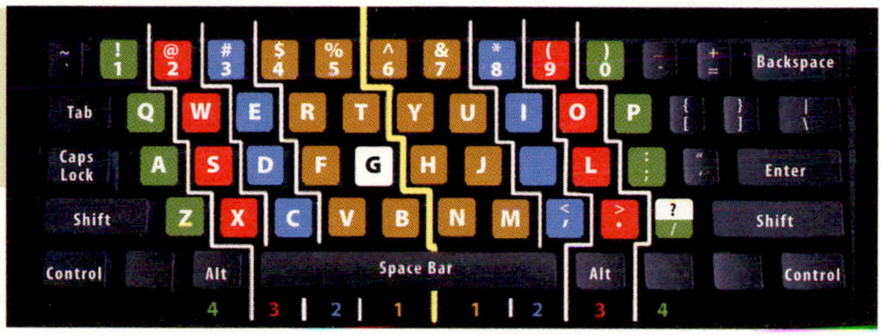

g Reach to *right* with *left first* finger.

? Left SHIFT; reach *down* with *right fourth* finger.

g

5 g g gf gaff gag grog fog frog drag cog dig fig gig
6 gf go gall flag gels slag gala gale glad glee gals
7 golf flog gorge glen high logs gore ogle page grow

? Go dig logs?

8 ? ?; ?; ? ? Who? When? Where? Who is? Who was?
9 Who is here? Was it he? Was it she? Did she go?
10 Did Geena? Did he? What is that? Was Jose here?

all reaches learned

11 Has Ginger lost her job? Was her April bill here?
12 Phil did not want the boats to get here this soon.
13 Loris Shin has been ill; Frank, a doctor, saw her.

8c Textbook Keying

Key each line once; DS between groups.

reach review
14 ws ws hj hj tf tf ol ol rf rf ed ed cd cd bf bf p;
15 wed bid has old hold rid heed heed car bed pot pot

g
16 gf gf gin gin rig ring go gone no nog sign got dog
17 to go | to go | go on | go in | go in | to go in | in the sign

One space after question mark.

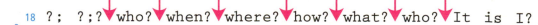

?
18 ?; ?;? who? when? where? how? what? who? It is I?
19 Is she? Is he? Did I lose Jo? Is Gal all right?

TECHNIQUE TIP

Concentrate on correct reaches.

DRILLS 9 AND 10

PERSONAL BUSINESS LETTER

1. Key the letter below following the Personal Business Letter Guidelines.
2. Save as *wp-drill9*.
3. Design and prepare a personal business letterhead for yourself. Use colors, fonts, and borders of your choice.
4. Save as *wp-drill10*.

Mark A. and Lauren C. Johnson

47 Mahalo Lane * Columbia, SC 29204-3380 * 803-555-0166 * Fax 803-555-0184 * Johnson@hotmail.com

2"

Current date ↓ 4

Mr. Joseph C. Holbrook
JH Safari Company
1240 N. Astor Street
Chicago, IL 60610-2308 ↓ 2

Dear Mr. Holbrook ↓ 2

Thank you for sending us the final itinerary and the preliminary documentation for our African safari. The revised itinerary is exactly what we expected, and we are especially pleased with the reservations made at both the camp on the Zambezi River in Zambia and the private game reserve in South Africa. ↓ 2

The preliminary documentation was very helpful. We have verified that our passports have more than six months prior to expiration and more than six blank pages. However, we have elected to wait and acquire the necessary visas at the borders of the countries requiring visas because it is easy to do and less expensive than using the service to acquire them prior to our departure. Our local physician has administered the required vaccinations, prescribed appropriate malaria prevention drugs, and provided us with signed copies of the International Certificate of Vaccination. ↓ 2

The enclosed travel form has been completed and signed. The medical and travel insurance information has been added to the form as requested. We look forward to receiving the final documentation and to having a wonderful experience on our first safari. ↓ 2

Sincerely ↓ 4

Lauren C. Johnson

Lauren C. Johnson ↓ 2

Enclosure

8d x and u

Key each line once; repeat.

x Reach *down* with *left third* finger.

your

u Reach *up* with *right first* finger.

x

20 x x xs xs ox ox lox sox fox box ex hex lax hex fax
21 sx six sax sox ax fix cox wax hex box pox sex text
22 flax next flex axel pixel exit oxen taxi axis next

u Use six guns?

23 u uj uj jug jut just dust dud due sue use due duel
24 uj us cud but bun out sun nut gun hut hue put fuel
25 dual laud dusk suds fuss full tuna tutus duds full

all reaches learned

26 Paige Power liked the book; Josh can read it next.
27 Next we picked a bag for Jan; then she, Jan, left.
28 Is her June account due? Has Lou ruined her unit?

Skill Building

8e Reinforcement

Key each line once; work for control.

29 nut cue hut sun rug us six cut dug axe rag fox run
30 out of the sun | cut the action | a fox den | fun at six
31 That car is not junk; it can run in the next race.

32 etc. tax nick cure lack flex walls uncle clad hurt
33 lack the cash | not just luck | next in line | just once
34 June Dunn can send that next tax case to Rex Knox.

8f Timed Writing

Take two 1' timings. If time permits, continue to paragraph 2. **Use wordwrap.**

TECHNIQUE TIP

Wordwrap: Text within a paragraph moves automatically to the next line. Tap ENTER only to begin a new paragraph.

Use wordwrap

4 8
How a finished job will look often depends on how
12 16 20
we feel about our work as we do it. Attitude has
24 28
a definite effect on the end result of work we do.

Tap ENTER once

4 8
When we are eager to begin a job, we relax and do
12 16 20
better work than if we start the job with an idea
24 28
that there is just nothing we can do to escape it.

Document Design

PERSONAL BUSINESS LETTER GUIDELINES

Personal business letters should adhere to the same general guidelines as business letters. Letters consist of three main parts: the opening lines to the receiver (date, letter address, and salutation), the body of the message, and the writer's closing lines (complimentary close, name, title, and enclosures if any). Standard letter parts are illustrated below.

Typically, personal business letters are prepared using block letter format with open punctuation. All letter parts are keyed at the left margin and punctuation is not used after the salutation or complimentary close.

Personal business letterhead can be easily designed using fonts, colors, and borders in the Open Screen of *Keyboarding Pro 6*. The letterhead shown has a .75" top margin, blue Vladimir Script 24-point font for the name followed by a 1/4-point blue line, and then blue Arial 9-point font for the address line.

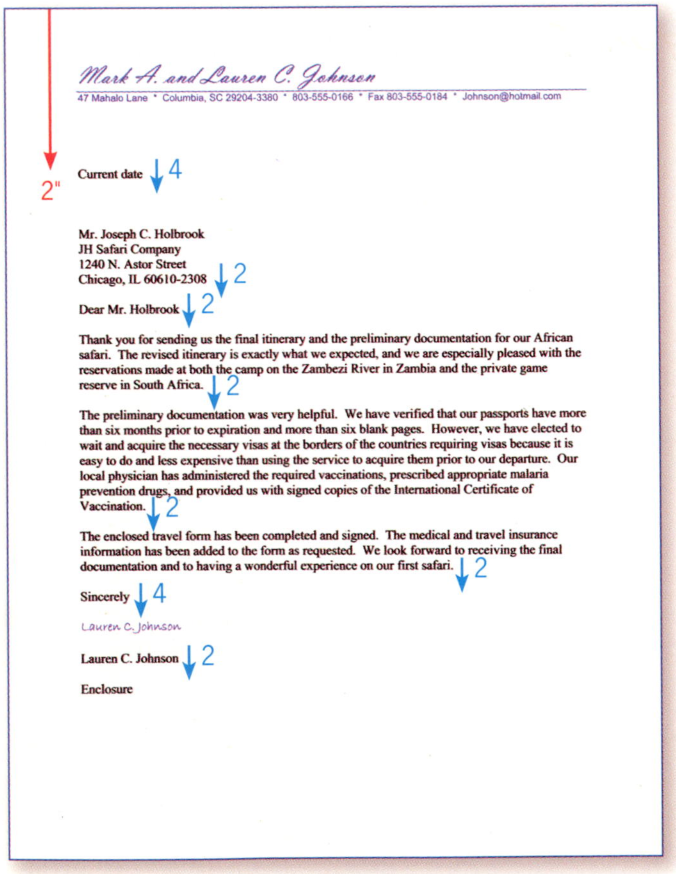

Mark A. and Lauren C. Johnson
47 Mahalo Lane • Columbia, SC 29204-3380 • 803-555-0166 • Fax 803-555-0184 • Johnson@hotmail.com

Current date

Mr. Joseph C. Holbrook
JH Safari Company
1240 N. Astor Street
Chicago, IL 60610-2308

Dear Mr. Holbrook

Thank you for sending us the final itinerary and the preliminary documentation for our African safari. The revised itinerary is exactly what we expected, and we are especially pleased with the reservations made at both the camp on the Zambezi River in Zambia and the private game reserve in South Africa.

The preliminary documentation was very helpful. We have verified that our passports have more than six months prior to expiration and more than six blank pages. However, we have elected to wait and acquire the necessary visas at the borders of the countries requiring visas because it is easy to do and less expensive than using the service to acquire them prior to our departure. Our local physician has administered the required vaccinations, prescribed appropriate malaria prevention drugs, and provided us with signed copies of the International Certificate of Vaccination.

The enclosed travel form has been completed and signed. The medical and travel insurance information has been added to the form as requested. We look forward to receiving the final documentation and to having a wonderful experience on our first safari.

Sincerely

Lauren C. Johnson

Lauren C. Johnson

Enclosure

Dateline: Date letters as of date prepared and position at 2" or at least 0.5" below the letterhead.

Letter Address: Include personal title, name, professional title (if known), company name, street address, city, state, and ZIP Code. Position four lines below date.

Salutation (or Greeting): Position two lines below the letter address and use a courtesy title (Mr., Ms., or Dr.). Use Ladies and Gentlemen when addressing a company. Do not use punctuation.

Body: Position two lines below the salutation.

Complimentary close: Position two lines below the body. Capitalize only the first letter. Do not use punctuation.

Signature: Writer should sign the letter or affix an electronic signature between the complimentary close and the writer's name.

Writer's Name: Position four lines below the complimentary close. Include a personal title to indicate gender only when the writer's name is not gender specific, such as Pat or Lynn or initials are used, and when the recipient does not know the writer.

Enclosure: Position an enclosure notation two lines below the writer's name if material is enclosed.

Lesson 9 | Q, M, V, Apostrophe

WARMUP

KEYBOARDING PRO DELUXE 2 — *Lessons/9a Warmup*

Key each line twice.

all letters 1 Lex gripes about cold weather; Fred is not joking.

space bar 2 Is it Di, Jo, or Al? Ask Lt. Coe, Bill; he knows.

easy 3 I did rush a bushel of cut corn to the sick ducks.

easy 4 He is to go to the Tudor Isle of England on a bus.

New Keys

9b q and m

Key each line once; repeat.

Queen Emma quips!

q Reach *up* with *left fourth* finger.

m Reach *down* with *right first* finger.

q

5 q qa qa quad quad quaff quant queen quo quit quick

6 qa qu qa quo quit quod quid quip quads quote quiet

7 quite quilts quart quill quakes quail quack quaint

m

8 m mj mj jam man malt mar max maw me mew men hem me

9 m mj ma am make male mane melt meat mist amen lame

10 malt meld hemp mimic tomb foam rams mama mire mind

all reaches learned

11 Quin had some quiet qualms about taming a macaque.

12 Jake Coxe had questions about a new floor program.

13 Max was quick to join the big reception for Lidia.

9c Textbook Keying

Key each line once for control. DS between 2-line groups.

m/x 14 me men ma am jam am lax, mix jam; the hem, six men

15 Emma Max expressed an aim to make a mammoth model.

DS

q/u 16 qa qu aqua aqua quit quit quip quite pro quo squad

17 Did Quin make a quick request to take the Qu exam?

DS

g/n 18 fg gn gun gun dig dig nag snag snag sign grab grab

19 Georgia hung a sign in front of the union for Gib.

DRILL 7

FORMATS, LINE SPACING, FONTS

1. Key the text without the character formats.
2. Save as *wp-drill7.*
3. Select the appropriate text and apply formats shown.
4. Select WEB APPS and apply 14-point font.
5. Save *wp-drill7* again and print. Do not close.
6. Select paragraphs 1 and 2 and apply Double Spacing.
7. Save as *wp-drill7r* and print.

WEB APPS

The word processor you are using to complete these activities is hosted by your computer. To use the word processor, you accessed it by clicking the *Word Processor* button in your ***Keyboarding Pro software***.

Similar word processors are hosted on the Internet. To access a word processor on the Internet, you use an <u>Internet connection</u> and a <u>Web browser</u>. These online word processors are generally called Web apps or Web applications.

DRILL 8

FORMATS, CENTER PAGE

1. Key the text applying the formats shown.
2. Center the page:
   a. Click the Format tab and then click Page Settings from the list of options on the menu.
   b. On the Page Parameters dialog box, in the Vertical Alignment box, click the down arrow and choose Center. Click OK.
3. Save as *wp-drill8*; print.

Center → WEB APPS

Align Left → Web apps provide both the word processor and storage space on the Internet. Documents stored on the Internet can be viewed and edited. New documents can also be created.

Justify → Documents stored on the Web can be accessed on the Internet with a browser at any time and from any location. Word processing software is not necessary on the computer used to access the documents. The two best-known word processing Web apps are listed below.

Center → *Google Docs*
Microsoft Office Web Apps

Align Right → For more information, contact:
Your Name
803-555-0126

9d V and ' (apostrophe)

Key each line once; repeat.

Apostrophe: The apostrophe shows (1) omission (as Rob't for Robert or it's for it is) or (2) possession when used with nouns (as Joe's hat).

© CENGAGE LEARNING

v Reach *down* with *left first* finger.

© CENGAGE LEARNING

' Reach to the *right* with the *right fourth* finger.

Viv votes.

v

```
20 v vf vf vie vie via via vim vat vow vile vale vote
21 vf vf ave vet ova eve vie dive five live have lave
22 cove dove over aver vivas hive volt five java jive
```

' (apostrophe)

Viv's vote counts.

```
23 '; '; it's it's Rod's; it's Bo's hat; we'll do it.
24 We don't know if it's Lee's pen or Norma's pencil.
25 It's ten o'clock; I won't tell him that he's late.
```

all reaches learned

```
26 It's Viv's turn to drive Iva's van to Ava's house.
27 Qua, not Vi, took the jet; so did Cal.  Didn't he?
28 Wasn't Fae Baxter a judge at the post garden show?
```

Skill Building

9e Reinforcement

Key each line once.

TECHNIQUE TIP

Keep your hands still as you reach to the third or bottom rows.

v/?

```
29 Viola said she has moved six times in five months.
30 Does Dave live on Vine Street?  Must he leave now?
```

q/?

```
31 Did Viv vote?  Can Paque move it?  Could Val dive?
32 Didn't Raquel quit Carl Quent after their quarrel?
```

direct reach

```
33 Fred told Brice that the junior class must depart.
34 June and Hunt decided to go to that great musical.
```

double letter

```
35 Harriette will cook dinner for the swimming teams.
36 Bill's committee meets in an accounting classroom.
```

9f Timed Writing

Key the paragraph once for control. Key it again a little faster. **Use wordwrap.**

Use wordwrap

We must be able to express our thoughts with ease if we desire to find success in the business world. It is there that sound ideas earn cash.

Character Formats

Sometimes you may want to emphasize or enhance the appearance of text. Attributes such as bold, underline, italic, fonts, and font sizes apply to characters. Use the Toolbar to access these formats. To be most efficient, key the text and then format it. To apply formats to text that has already been keyed, select the text and click the appropriate format button.

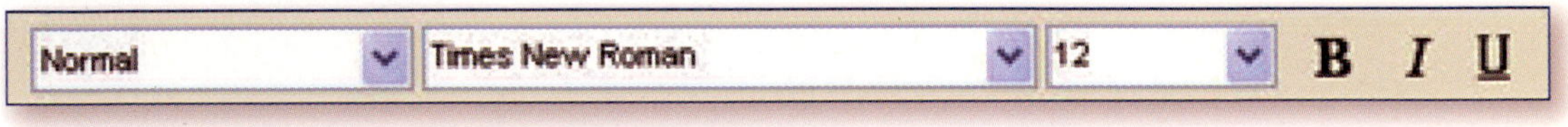

Paragraph Formats

Each time you tap ENTER, the word processor inserts a paragraph mark (¶) and starts a new paragraph. A paragraph may consist of a single line followed by a hard return (¶ mark) or several lines that wrap and are followed by a hard return. Paragraph formats include alignment, line spacing, and tabs. To view hard returns or paragraphs, choose **View** menu, **Show codes**.

Paragraph formats such as alignment, tabs, and line spacing apply to an entire paragraph. Paragraph formats can be applied to existing text by selecting the text and applying the format. To apply a paragraph format as you key, select the format and key the text. The feature will be "turned on" until you click the turn it off.

Alignment

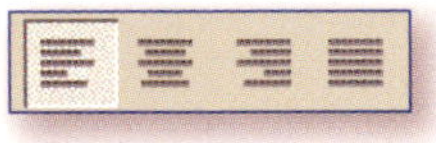

The alignment commands are located on the toolbar and include: Align Left, Center, Align Right, and Justify. To align existing text, select the text and apply the format. Alignment is a paragraph command.

Line Spacing

The default line spacing is single; to change line spacing, position the insertion point in the paragraph you wish to change. Click the Format tab on the menu bar and select Paragraph; then click Double Space. To change multiple paragraphs, select the paragraphs first.

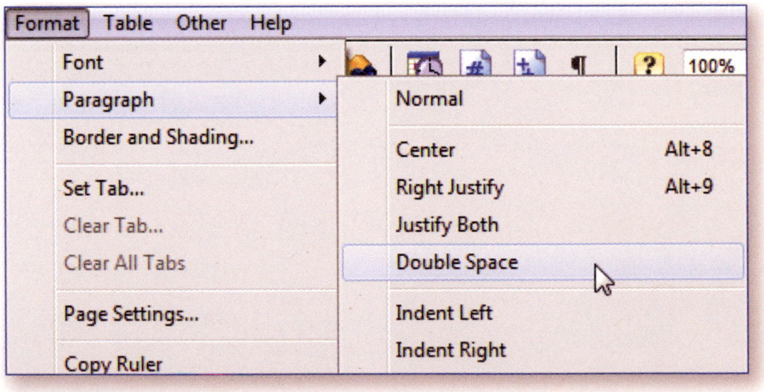

DRILL 6

FORMATS

1. Key each of the sentences, applying the format as you key. Save as *wp-drill6*. Print.
2. Clear the screen (click the New button).

1. **These words are keyed in bold.**
2. *These words are keyed in italic.*
3. <u>These words are underlined.</u>
4. This line is keyed in 14 point.

Lesson 10 | *Z, Y, Quotation Mark, Tab*

WARMUP

KEYBOARDING PRO DELUXE 2

Lessons/10a Warmup

Key each line twice.

all letters 1 Quill owed those back taxes after moving to Japan.
spacing 2 Didn't Vi, Sue, and Paul go? Someone did; I know.
q/v/m 3 Marv was quite quick to remove that mauve lacquer.
easy 4 Lana is a neighbor; she owns a lake and an island.

New Keys

10b z and y

Key each line once; repeat.

Zig zag to jazz.

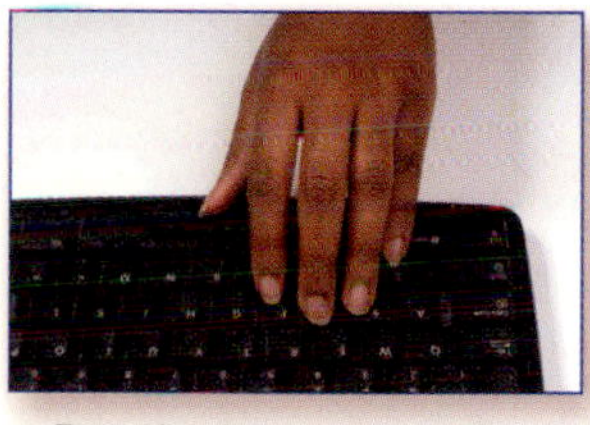

z Reach *down* with *left fourth* finger.

z

5 za za zap zap zing zig zag zoo zed zip zap zig zed
6 doze zeal zero haze jazz zone zinc zing size ozone
7 ooze maze doze zoom zarf zebus daze gaze faze adze

y Say yes to Ziggy.

8 y yj yj jay jay hay hay lay nay say days eyes ayes
9 yj ye yet yen yes cry dry you rye sty your fry wry
10 ye yen bye yea coy yew dye yaw lye yap yak yon any

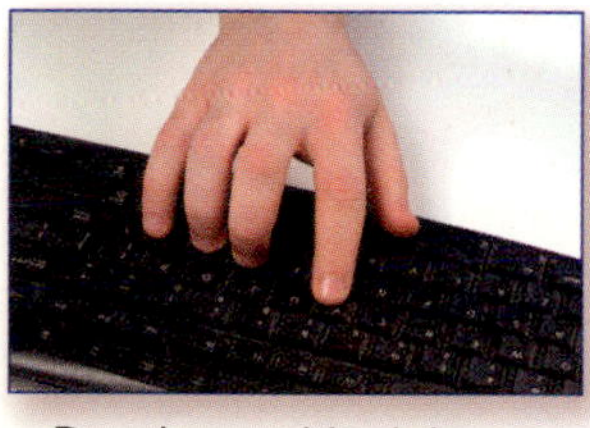

y Reach *up* with *right first* finger.

all reaches learned

11 Did you say Liz saw any yaks or zebus at your zoo?
12 Relax; Jake wouldn't acquire any favorable rights.
13 Has Mazie departed? Tex, Lu, and I will go alone.

10c Textbook Keying

Key each line once. DS between groups.

14 Cecilia brings my jumbo umbrella to every concert.
direct reach 15 John and Kim recently brought us an old art piece.
16 I built a gray brick border around my herb garden.

DS

17 sa ui hj gf mn vc ew uy re io as lk rt jk df op yu
adjacent reach 18 In Ms. Lopez' opinion, the opera was really great.
19 Polly and I were joining Walker at the open house.

Insert/Delete

Insert and Delete features are used to correct errors or revise documents.

Insert: To insert text, simply position the insertion point at the location where the new text is to appear and key the text. Existing text moves to the right.

Delete: The DELETE key erases text that is no longer needed.

To delete a character: Position the insertion point to the left of the character to delete and tap DELETE or position the insertion point to the right of the character to delete and tap BACKSPACE. Be careful not to hold down the delete or backspace keys since they will continue to erase characters.

To delete a word: Double-click the word to be deleted and tap DELETE.

Select

Select identifies text that has been keyed so that it can be modified. Selected text appears black on the screen. Select text using the mouse.

To select text	Position the insertion point on the first character to be selected. Click the left mouse button and drag the mouse over the text to be selected. To deselect after each item click the mouse again.
To select a word	Double-click the word.
To select a paragraph	Triple-click in the paragraph.
To select multiple lines	Click the left mouse button and drag in the area left of the lines.

DRILL 5

EDIT TEXT

1. Make the deletions shown at the right. (Your document will be single-spaced.)
2. Correct any other errors you may have made.
3. Save as *wp-drill5*.
4. Click the Print button on the toolbar.
5. Use the mouse to select each of the following items. Deselect after each item.
   - The first sentence.
   - The word Serendipity in paragraph 1.
   - All of paragraph 1.
   - The entire document.
6. Move the insertion point to the beginning of the document. Key your name at the left margin. Tap ENTER four times. Do not save or print.

Serendipity, a ~~new homework~~ research tool from Information Technology Company, is available to subscribers of ~~the major~~ online services via the World Wide Web.

Offered as a subscription service aimed at ~~college~~ students, Serendipity is a collection of tens of thousands of articles from ~~major~~ encyclopedias, reference books, magazines, pamphlets, and Internet sources combined into a single searchable database.

Serendipity puts an electronic library right at students' fingertips ^with just a computer and an Internet connection. The program offers two browse-and-search capabilities. Users can find articles ^on just about any subject by entering questions in simple question format or browse the database by pointing and clicking on key words that identify related articles. For more information, call ^1-800-555-0174 or address e-mail to <<lab@serendipity.com>>.

10d " (quotation mark) and TAB

Key each line once; repeat.

© CENGAGE LEARNING

TAB Reach *up* with *left fourth* finger.

© CENGAGE LEARNING

" Shift; then reach to the *right* with the *right fourth* finger.

" (quotation mark)

20 "; "; " " "lingo" "bugs" "tennies" I like "malts."

21 "I am not," she said, "going." I just said, "Oh?"

tab key

22 The tab key is used for indenting paragraphs and aligning columns.

23 Tabs that are set by the software are called default tabs, which are usually a half inch.

Skill Building

10e Textbook Keying

Key lines 24–30 once. Tap TAB to indent each paragraph. Use wordwrap, tapping ENTER only at the end of each paragraph.

24 The expression "I give you my word," or put another
25 way, "Take my word for it," is just a way I can say, "I
26 prize my name; it clearly stands in back of my words."
27 I offer "honor" as collateral.

tab 28 Tap the tab key and begin the line without a pause to maintain fluency.

29 She said that this is the lot to be sent; I agreed with her.

30 Tap Tab before starting to key a timed writing so that the first line is indented.

10f Timed Writing

Take two 1' timings beginning with paragraph 1. If you finish before time is up, continue with paragraph 2. **Use wordwrap.**

Goal: 15 *gwam*

TECHNIQUE TIP

Wordwrap: Text within a paragraph moves automatically to the next line. Tap ENTER only to begin a new paragraph.

wordwrap

gwam 1'

Tab → All of us work for progress, but it is not 8
always easy to analyze "progress." We work hard 18
for it; but, in spite of some really good efforts, 28
we may fail to receive just exactly the response we 39
want. 40

Tab → When this happens, as it does to all of us, 9
it is time to cease whatever we are doing, have 18
a quiet talk with ourselves, and face up to the 28
questions about our limited progress. How can we 38
do better? 40

| 1 | 2 | 3 | 4 | 5 | 6 | 7 | 8 | 9 | 10 |

Help

Use the Help button to answer questions you may have about the software.

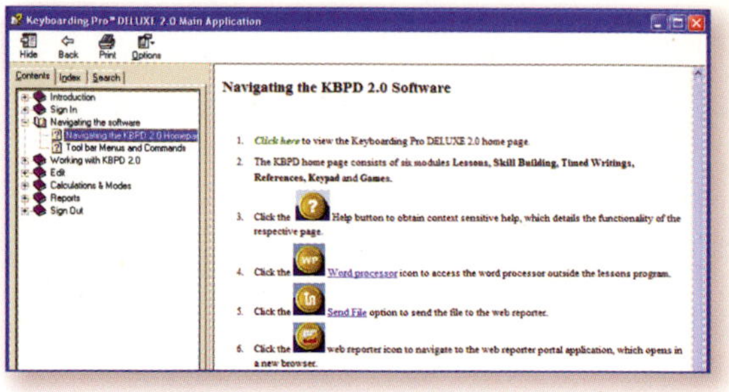

DRILL 1

FILE, EDIT, AND FORMAT TABS ON MENU BAR

1. Click the File tab on the Menu bar. Observe the items on the File menu.
2. Click Open to display the Open dialog box; click Cancel to close it.
3. Click the Edit tab on the Menu bar; view the items listed.
4. Click the Format tab to view the Format menu.

DRILL 2

HELP AND PRINT

1. Click the Help tab on the Menu bar, then Help Topics.
2. Select Navigating the software and click Navigating the KBPD 2.0 Homepage.
3. Use the Scroll bar to view all of the information.
4. Click the Print command at the top of the Help dialog box to print the information.

DRILL 3

INSERT TAB ON MENU BAR

1. Click the Insert tab on the Menu bar, then select Symbol.
2. Select the Special Characters tab and view the options.
3. Click Done to close the Symbol dialog box.

DRILL 4

CREATE PARAGRAPH

1. Key the paragraph.
2. Click the Save button. Key **wp drill4** in the File name box.
3. Click the New button. You now have a clear screen.
4. Click Open button. Click *drill-4* then OK to open Drill 4.
5. Position the insertion point at the beginning of Sentence 2. Tap ENTER. You now have three paragraphs.
6. Continue to Drill 5. Do not exit this document.

Serendipity, a new homework research tool from Information Technology Company, is available to subscribers of the major online services via the World Wide Web. Offered as a subscription service aimed at college students, Serendipity is a collection of tens of thousands of articles from major encyclopedias, reference books, magazines, pamphlets, and Internet sources combined into a single searchable database.

Serendipity puts an electronic library right at students' fingertips. The program offers two browse-and-search capabilities. Users can find articles by entering questions in simple question format or browse the database by pointing and clicking on key words that identify related articles. For more information, call 800-555-0174 or address e-mail to <<lab@serendipity.com>>.

Lesson 11 | Review

WARMUP

KEYBOARDING PRO DELUXE 2

Lessons/11a Warmup

Key line twice (slowly, then faster).

alphabet 1 Zeb had Jewel quickly give him five or six points.
" (quote) 2 Can you spell "chaos," "bias," "bye," and "their"?
y 3 Ty Clay may envy you for any zany plays you write.
easy 4 Did he bid on the bicycle, or did he bid on a map?
| 1 | 2 | 3 | 4 | 5 | 6 | 7 | 8 | 9 | 10 |

Skill Building

11b Keyboard Reinforcement

Key each line once; repeat the drill to increase fluency.

TECHNIQUE TIP

Work for smoothness, not speed.

5 za za zap az az maze zoo zip razz zed zax zoa zone
6 Liz Zahl saw Zoe feed the zebra in an Arizona zoo.

7 yj yj jy jy joy lay yaw say yes any yet my try you
8 Why do you say that today, Thursday, is my payday?

9 xs xs sax ox box fix hex ax lax fox taxi lox sixes
10 Roxy, you may ask Jay to fix any tax sets for you.

11 qa qa aqua quail quit quake quid equal quiet quart
12 Did Enrique quietly but quickly quell the quarrel?

13 fv fv five lives vow ova van eve avid vex vim void
14 Has Vivi, Vada, or Eva visited Vista Valley Farms?

11c Speed Builders

Key each balanced-hand line twice, as quickly as you can.

15 is to for do an may work so it but an with them am
16 am yam map aid zig yams ivy via vie quay cob amend

17 to do is for an may work so it but am an with them
18 for it|for it|to the|to the|do they|do they|do it

19 Pamela may go to the farm with Jan and a neighbor.
20 Rod and Ty may go by the lake if they go downtown.
| 1 | 2 | 3 | 4 | 5 | 6 | 7 | 8 | 9 | 10 |

Word Processing

Word Processor WP

KEYBOARDING PRO

You can use the *Keyboarding Pro 6* Word Processor to practice keyboarding skills, create a letter, or take a timed writing. To access the word processor, click the button shown at the left. The word processor's formatting capabilities include:

- Fonts
- Styles
- Sizes
- Margins
- Tabs
- Justification
- Line Spacing
- Insert Pictures
- Insert Symbols
- Insert Tables

Note in Figure 1 that it is a *Windows*' word processor, so it is similar to *Microsoft Word*.

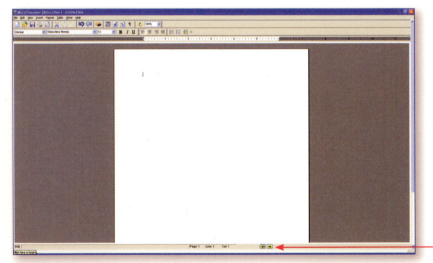

Timer

Figure 1 Word Processor Open Screen

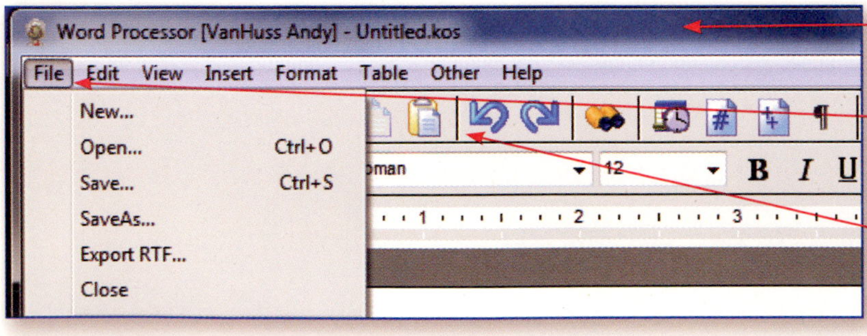

Title bar: Displays the name of the application and the document that is currently open.

Tabs: Each tab on the menu bar displays a menu of commands that you will use to create, edit, and format documents.

Toolbar: Provides shortcuts to many of the commands in the word processor.

Figure 2 Ribbon and Menu of Commands

Figure 3 Word Processor Timer

Timer: Click the Timer button on the Status bar at the bottom of the Word Processor screen to take a timed writing. Set the timer for 15" or 30" or for 1', 3', or 5'. The timing begins once you start to key and stops automatically.

11d Textbook Keying

Key each line once. Tap ENTER at the end of each line. DS between the groups of lines.

★ TECHNIQUE TIP

Tap CAPS LOCK to capitalize several letters. Tap it again to toggle CAPS LOCK off.

enter: key smoothly without looking at fingers

21 Make the return snappily
22 and with assurance; keep
23 your eyes on your source
24 data; maintain a smooth,
25 constant pace as you key.

DS

© CENGAGE LEARNING

space bar: use down-and-in motion

26 us me it of he an by do go to us if or so am ah el
27 Have you a pen? If so, print "Free to any guest."

DS

caps lock: press to toggle it on or off

28 Use ALL CAPS for items such as TO, FROM, or SUBJECT.
29 Did Kristin mean Kansas City, MISSOURI, or KANSAS?

11e Timed Writing

1. Take two 2' timings on all paragraphs. If you finish before time is up, start over with paragraph 1. Use wordwrap. Key fluently but with control. **Use wordwrap.**

   Goal: 16 *gwam*

2. End the lesson but do not exit the software.

To determine gross-words-a-minute (*gwam*) rate for 2':

Follow these steps if you are *not* using *Keyboarding Pro*.

1. Note the figure at the end of the last line completed.
2. For a partial line, note the figure on the scale direcly below the point at which you stopped keying.
3. Add these two figures to determine the total gross words a minute (*gwam*) you keyed.

	gwam	2'
Have we thought of communication as a kind	4	31
of war that we wage through each day?	8	35
When we think of it that way, good language	12	39
would seem to become our major line of attack.	17	44
Words become muscle; in a normal exchange or in	22	49
a quarrel, we do well to realize the power of words.	27	54

11f Enrichment

1. Click the Skill Building tab from the main menu and choose Technique Builder; select Drill 1a.
2. Key Drill 1a from page 31. Key each line once striving for good accuracy.
3. The results will be listed on the Skill Building Report.

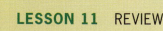

DRILL 5

Review

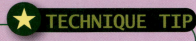

TECHNIQUE TIP

Keep fingers curved and upright over home keys. Keep right thumb tucked under palm.

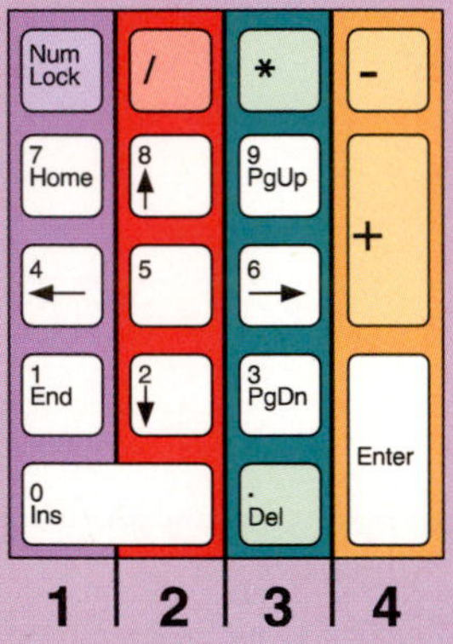

a	b	c	d	e	f
349	854	961	789	631	80
64	97	164	64	972	167
108	326	207	207	803	549
25	40	83	153	54	23

a	b	c	d	e	f
51	467	825	347	901	208
873	54	258	540	467	375
106	208	504	45	95	34
24	13	13	126	238	160
94	648	21	52	178	341
157	72	341	412	57	89

a	b	c	d	e	f
687	645	32	87	461	541
21	58	647	281	38	1,923
2,753	1,002	549	105	20	567
3,054	25	4,008	2,194	3,079	2,089
369	4,770	158	3,066	657	478
1,004	123	2,560	38	2,098	3,257

a	b	c	d	e	f
71.64	2.72	27.59	89.24	4.02	.57
285.36	118.50	438.96	102.46	55.71	6.37
3.79	24.73	4.71	527.90	.64	1.27

a	b	c	d	e	f
42.08	63.87	91.47	159.34	28.47	1.25
31.07	128.46	1.50	.28	374.95	116.00
365.87	.24	163.48	22.84	24.96	514.38
.25	394.28	452.87	349.51	852.43	234.94
147.25	32.54	821.47	164.87	.08	3.54
183.12	20.80	.60	5.07	121.07	.97

Lesson 12 | Review

WARMUP

KEYBOARDING PRO DELUXE 2 — *Lessons/12a Warmup*

Key each line twice (slowly, then faster).

alphabet 1 Jack won five quiz games; Brad will play him next.
q 2 Quin Racq quickly and quietly quelled the quarrel.
z 3 Zaret zipped along sizzling, zigzag Arizona roads.
easy 4 Did he hang the sign by the big bush at the lake?
| 1 | 2 | 3 | 4 | 5 | 6 | 7 | 8 | 9 | 10 |

Skill Building

12b New Key Review

Key each line once; DS between groups. Work for smoothness, not speed.

b/f
5 bf bf fab fab ball bib rf rf rib rib fibs bums bee
6 Did Buffy remember that he is a brass band member?

z/y
7 za za zag zig zip yj yj jay eye day lazy hazy zest
8 Liz amazed us with the zesty pizza on a lazy trip.

q/u
9 qa qa quo qt. quit quay quad quarm que uj jug quay
10 Where is Quito? Qatar? Boqueirao? Quebec? Quilmes?

v/m
11 vf vf valve five value mj mj ham mad mull mass vim
12 Vito, enter the words vim, vivace, and avar; save.

all
13 I faced defeat; only reserves saved my best crews.
14 In my opinion, I need to rest in my reserved seat.

all
15 Holly created a red poppy and deserves art awards.
16 My pump averages a faster rate; we get better oil.

12c Textbook Keying

Key each line once; DS between groups. Work for smooth, unhurried keying.

de/ed
17 ed fed led deed dell dead deal sled desk need seed
18 Dell dealt with the deed before the dire deadline.

ol/lo
19 old tolls doll solo look sole lost love cold stole
20 Old Ole looked for the long lost olive oil lotion.

op/po
21 pop top post rope pout port stop opal opera report
22 Stop to read the top opera opinion report to Opal.

we/ew
23 we few wet were went wears weather skews stew blew
24 Working women wear sweaters when weather dictates.

TECHNIQUE TIP

Keep fingers curved and body aligned properly.

DRILL 4

Decimal

Follow the directions given. The decimal (.) key is usually located at the bottom right of the keypad. Use the third finger to reach down to tap the decimal key.

TECHNIQUE TIP

Tap each key with a quick, sharp stroke. Release the key quickly. Keep the fingers curved and upright, the wrist low and relaxed.

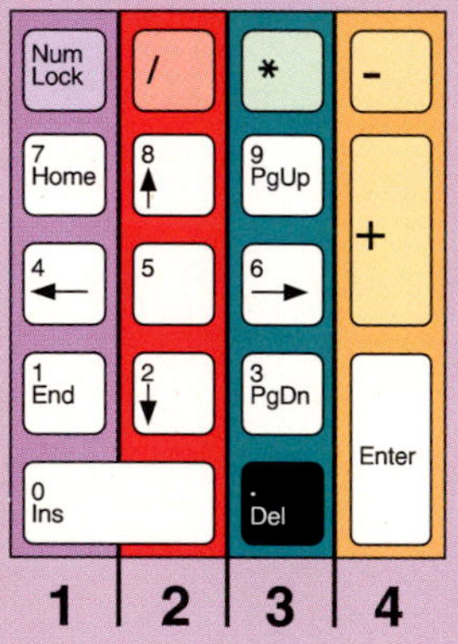

a	b	c	d	e	f
.28	.19	.37	.42	.81	.96
.51	.67	.81	.27	.55	.80
.64	.50	.60	.50	.62	.43
7.10	8.91	5.64	3.12	6.04	5.01
5.32	4.27	9.21	6.47	5.28	3.24
8.94	3.06	7.38	5.89	1.37	6.78
3.62	36.94	86.73	.60	8.21	4.02
8.06	10.31	537.34	5.21	100.89	6.51
321.04	10.55	687.52	164.84	.85	207.65
.75	.26	10.85	627.98	2.57	46.51
687.46	357.95	159.46	85.21	654.32	753.15
20.46	220.48	6.10	3.04	123.54	315.47
761.64	2.82	627.25	196.25	82.99	4.02
285.46	34.60	.29	89.24	512.69	99.80
33.99	739.45	290.23	563.21	701.21	546.78
60.41	52.79	105.87	951.32	357.02	123.94
108.97	211.00	46.24	82.47	61.28	75.61
3.54	5.79	5.41	1.32	8.54	.27
.05	1.19	77.54	112.96	33.68	2.75
112.54	561.34	114.85	.24	647.21	432.89
35.67	22.01	67.90	41.08	71.28	11.00
579.21	105.24	731.98	258.96	741.21	546.21
.34	1.68	.24	.87	.63	.54
21.87	54.89	2.34	5.89	4.68	10.72

12d Textbook Keying

Key each line once; DS between 3-line groups. Concentrate and key with control.

TECHNIQUE TIP

Keep hands quiet; do not bounce. Keep fingers curved and upright.

```
25 a for we you is that be this will be a to and well
26 as our with I or a to by your form which all would
27 new year no order they so new but now year who may
                                                     DS
28 This is Lyn's only date to visit their great city.
29 I can send it to your office at any time you wish.
30 She kept the fox, owls, and fowl down by the lake.
                                                     DS
31 Harriette will cook dinner for the swimming teams.
32 Annette will call at noon to give us her comments.
33 Johnny was good at running and passing a football.
   | 1 | 2 | 3 | 4 | 5 | 6 | 7 | 8 | 9 | 10 |
```

12e Timed Writing

Key a 2' timing on both paragraphs. If you finish before time is up, start again with paragraph 1. Key fluently but not rushed. Repeat the timing again for 2'. **Use wordwrap.**

Goal: 16 *gwam*

Copy Difficulty

What factors determine whether copy is difficult or easy? Research shows that difficulty is influenced by syllables per word, characters per word, and percent of familiar words. Carefully controlling these three factors ensures that speed and accuracy scores are reliable—that is, increased scores reflect increased skill.

In Level 1, all timings are easy. Note "E" inside the triangle at left of the timing. Easy timings contain an average of 1.2 syllables per word, 5.1 characters per word, and 90 percent familiar words. Easy copy is suitable for the beginner who is mastering the keyboard.

E **ALL LETTERS**

```
                        •        4        •       8      gwam 2'
      There should be no questions, no doubt, about        5 | 35
  •       12        •        16        •
the value of being able to key; it's just a matter        10 | 40
   20        •        24        •       28       •
of common sense that today a pencil is much too slow.     15 | 45
                 •         4         •       8
      Let me explain.  Work is done on a keyboard          19 | 49
     •          12          •          16        •
three to six times faster than other writing and          24 | 54
        20         •         24        •       28
with a product that is a prize to read.  Don't you        29 | 59
     •
agree?                                                    30 | 60
2' |   1   |   2   |   3   |   4   |   5   |
```

DRILL 3

1, 2, 3

Complete Lesson 3 before keying Drill 3.

TECHNIQUE TIP

Keep fingers curved and upright over home keys. Keep right thumb tucked under palm.

© CENGAGE LEARNING

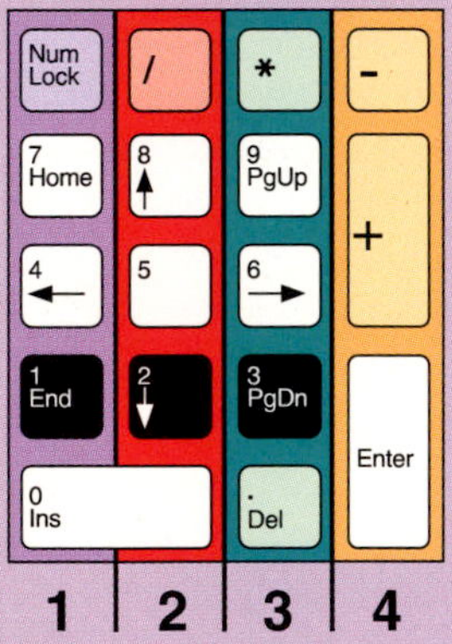

a	b	c	d	e	f
11	22	33	14	15	16
41	52	63	36	34	35
24	26	25	22	42	62
27	18	39	30	20	10
30	30	10	19	61	43
32	31	21	53	83	71

414	141	525	252	636	363
141	111	252	222	363	333
111	414	222	525	333	636

111	141	222	252	366	336
152	342	624	141	243	121
330	502	331	302	110	432
913	823	721	633	523	511
702	612	513	712	802	823
213	293	821	813	422	722

24	36	15	12	32	34
115	334	226	254	346	246
20	140	300	240	105	304
187	278	347	159	357	158
852	741	963	654	321	987
303	505	819	37	92	10

28	91	37	22	13	23
524	631	423	821	922	733
15	221	209	371	300	25
823	421	24	31	19	107
652	813	211	354	231	187
50	31	352	16	210	30

Lesson 13 | Review

WARMUP

KEYBOARDING PRO DELUXE 2 — *Lessons/13a Warmup*

Key each line twice (slowly, then faster).

alphabet 1 Bev quickly hid two Japanese frogs in Mitzi's box.
shift 2 Jay Nadler, a Rotary Club member, wrote Mr. Coles.
, (comma) 3 Jay, Ed, and I paid for plates, knives, and forks.
easy 4 Did the amendment name a city auditor to the firm?

| 1 | 2 | 3 | 4 | 5 | 6 | 7 | 8 | 9 | 10 |

Skill Building

13b Textbook Keying

Key each line once; DS between groups of lines. Key the text as suggested:

Lines 5–7: Key the words as a single unit.

Lines 8–10: Key the words letter by letter.

Lines 11–13: Vary your keying as your fingers find the right rhythm.

word-level response: key short, familiar words as units

5 is to for do an may work so it but an with them am
6 Did they mend the torn right half of their ensign?
7 Hand me the ivory tusk on the mantle by the bugle.

letter-level response: key more difficult words letter by letter

8 only state jolly zest oil verve join rate mop card
9 After defeat, look up; gaze in joy at a few stars.
10 We gazed at a plump beaver as it waded in my pool.

combination response: use variable speed; your fingers will let you feel the difference

11 it up so at for you may was but him work were they
12 It is up to you to get the best rate; do it right.
13 Sami greeted reporters as stars got ready at home.

| 1 | 2 | 3 | 4 | 5 | 6 | 7 | 8 | 9 | 10 |

13c Keyboard Reinforcement

Key each line once; fingers well curved, wrists low.

p 14 Pat appears happy to pay for any supper I prepare.
x 15 Knox can relax; Alex gets a box of flax next week.
v 16 Vi, Ava, and Viv move ivy vines, leaves, or stems.
' 17 It's a question of whether they can't or won't go.
? 18 Did Jan go? Did she see Ray? Who paid? Did she?
. 19 Ms. E. K. Nu and Lt. B. A. Walz had the a.m. duty.
" 20 "Who are you?" he asked. "I am," I said, "Marie."
; 21 Find a car; try it; like it; work a price; buy it.

DRILL 2

7, 8, 9

Complete Lesson 2 before keying Drill 2.

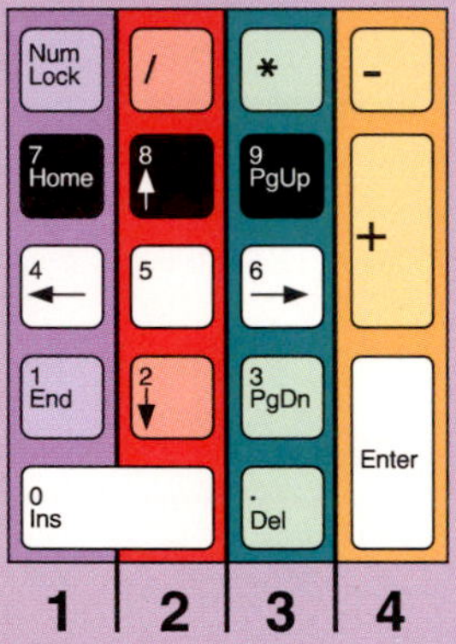

a	b	c	d	e	f
74	85	96	70	80	90
47	58	96	87	78	98
90	70	80	90	90	70
89	98	78	89	77	87
86	67	57	48	68	57
59	47	48	67	58	69

470	580	690	770	707	407
999	969	888	858	474	777
777	474	888	585	999	696

858	969	747	770	880	990
757	858	959	857	747	678
579	849	879	697	854	796
857	967	864	749	864	795
609	507	607	889	990	448
597	847	449	457	684	599

85	74	96	98	78	88
957	478	857	994	677	579
657	947	479	76	94	795
887	965	789	577	649	849
90	80	70	806	709	407
407	567	494	97	80	70

50	790	807	90	75	968
408	97	66	480	857	57
87	479	567	947	808	970
690	85	798	587	907	89
94	754	879	67	594	847
489	880	97	907	69	579

13d Textbook Keying

Troublesome Pairs: Key each line once; DS between groups.

© CENGAGE LEARNING

© CENGAGE LEARNING

TECHNIQUE TIP

Keep hands and arms still as you reach up to the third row and down to the first row.

```
t 22   at fat hat sat to tip the that they fast last slat
r 23   or red try ran run air era fair rid ride trip trap
t/r 24 A trainer sprained an arm trying to tame the bear.
                                                      DS
m 25   am me my mine jam man more most dome month minimum
n 26   no an now nine once net knee name ninth know never
m/n 27 Many men and women are important company managers.
                                                      DS
o 28   on or to not now one oil toil over only solo today
i 29   it is in tie did fix his sit like with insist will
o/i 30 Joni will consider obtaining options to buy coins.
                                                      DS
a 31   at an as art has and any case data haze tart smart
s 32   us as so say sat slap lass class just sassy simple
a/s 33 Disaster was averted as the steamer sailed to sea.
                                                      DS
e 34   we he ear the key her hear chef desire where there
i 35   it is in tie did fix his sit like with insist will
e/i 36 An expression of gratitude for service is desired.
```

13e Timed Writing

Key a 2' writing on both paragraphs. If you finish before time is up, start again with paragraph 1. Key fluently but not rushed. Repeat the timing again for 2'. **Use wordwrap.**

Goal: 16 *gwam*

E ALL LETTERS

	gwam 2'
The questions of time use are vital ones; we	5
miss so much just because we don't plan.	9
When we organize our days, we save time for	13
those extra premium things we long to do.	17

2' | 1 | 2 | 3 | 4 | 5 |

DRILL 1

4, 5, 6, 0

Complete Lesson 1 before keying Drill 1.

1. Turn on NUMLOCK. Click the Keypad Practice button.
2. Tap ENTER after each number.
3. To obtain a total, tap ENTER twice after the last number in a group.
4. Key each problem until the same answer is obtained twice; you can then be reasonably sure that you have the correct answer.

Follow these directions for each lesson.

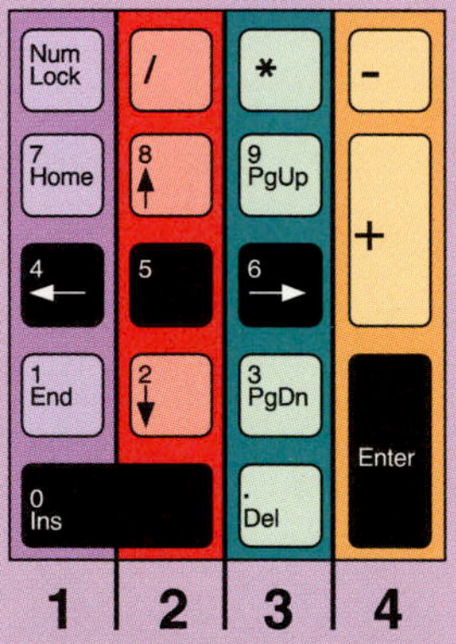

© CENGAGE LEARNING

a	b	c	d	e	f
46	55	56	46	55	56
45	64	45	45	64	45
66	56	64	66	56	64
56	44	65	56	44	65
54	65	45	54	65	45
65	54	44	65	54	44
466	445	546	654	465	665
564	654	465	545	446	645
456	464	546	545	564	456
556	544	644	466	644	646
644	455	464	654	464	554
454	546	565	554	456	656
400	404	505	606	500	600
404	505	606	500	600	400
500	600	400	404	505	606
650	506	404	550	440	550
506	460	605	460	604	640
406	500	640	504	460	560
504	640	550	440	660	406
560	450	650	450	505	550
640	504	440	640	450	660
400	600	500	500	600	400
650	505	404	606	540	560
504	404	640	404	406	606

Skill Builder 1

KEYBOARDING PRO DELUXE 2 | **Skill Building** | *Technique Builder*

From the Skill Building tab, select Technique Builder and then the drill. Key each line once at a comfortable rate. Tap ENTER at the end of each line. Single-space the drill. Concentrate and key accurately. Repeat if desired.

DRILL 1

Goal: reinforce key locations

Key each line once at a comfortable, constant rate.

TECHNIQUE TIP

Keep
- your eyes on source copy
- your fingers curved, upright
- your wrists low but not touching
- your elbows hanging loosely
- your feet flat on the floor

Drill 1a

A We saw that Alan had an alabaster vase in Alabama.
B My rubber boat bobbed about in the bubbling brook.
C Ceci gave cups of cold cocoa to Rebecca and Rocco.
D Don's dad added a second deck to his old building.
E Even as Ellen edited her document, she ate dinner.
F Our firm in Buffalo has a staff of forty or fifty.
G Ginger is giving Greg the eggs she got from Helga.
H Hugh has eighty high, harsh lights he might flash.

Drill 1b

I Irik's lack of initiative is irritating his coach.
J Judge J. J. Jore rejected Jeane and Jack's jargon.
K As a lark, Kirk kicked back a rock at Kim's kayak.
L Lucille is silly; she still likes lemon lollipops.
M Milt Mumm hammered a homer in the Miami home game.
N Ken Linn has gone hunting; Stan can begin canning.
O Jon Soto rode off to Otsego in an old Morgan auto.
P Philip helped pay the prize as my puppy hopped up.
Q Quiet Raquel quit quoting at an exquisite marquee.

Drill 1c

R As Mrs. Kerr's motor roared, her red horse reared.
S Sissie lives in Mississippi; Lissa lives in Tulsa.
T Nat told Betty not to tattle on her little sister.
U Ula has a unique but prudish idea on unused units.
V Eva visited every vivid event for twelve evenings.
W We watched as wayworn wasps swarmed by the willow.
X Tex Cox waxed the next box for Xenia and Rex Knox.
Y Ty says you may stay with Fay for only sixty days.
Z Hazel is puzzled about the azure haze; Zack dozes.

Numeric Keypad

Skill Building

Keypad Lessons

Keypad instruction is available from the Keypad tab in *Keyboarding Pro 6*. The NUMLOCK key must be on for you to use the software. The Summary Report shows the exercise you have completed and the scores achieved. Complete each lesson before keying the related practice on the next few pages.

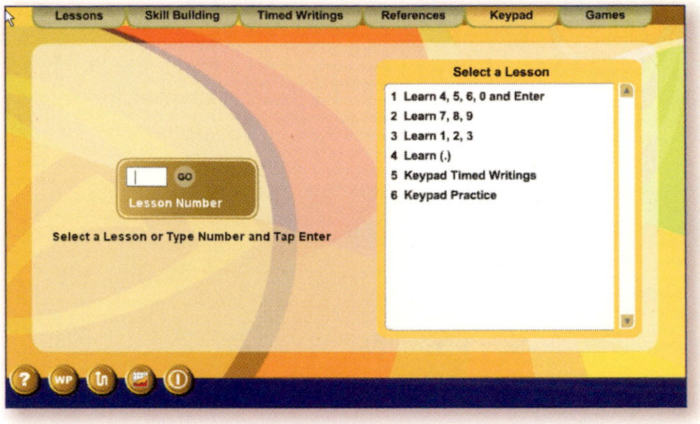

Keypad Timed Writings

Select Keypad Analysis on the Keypad lesson menu for additional keypad practice. Nine activities are available, each of which emphasizes a certain row or number type.

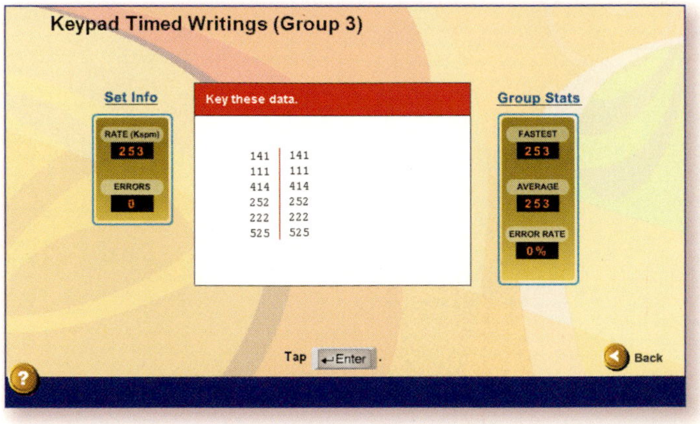

Keypad Practice

Select the Keypad Practice button to practice the exercises on the next few pages. Tap ENTER on the keypad after each number. Tap ENTER twice to sum the amounts keyed. Click the Print button to print the figures.

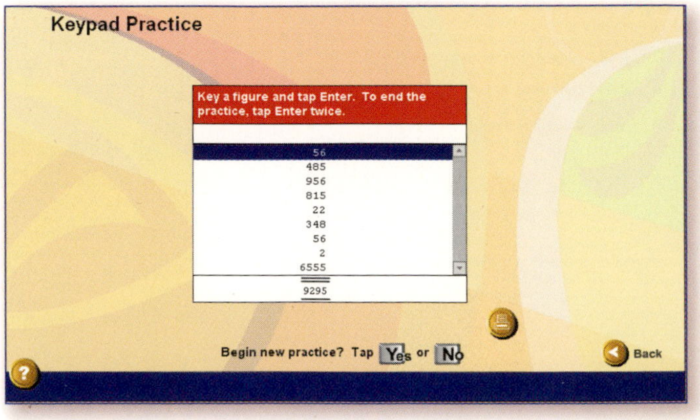

DRILL 2

Goal: strengthen up and down reaches

Keep hands and wrists quiet; fingers well curved in home position; stretch fingers up from home or pull them palmward as needed.

home position

1 Hall left for Dallas; he is glad Jake fed his dog.
2 Ada had a glass flask; Jake had a sad jello salad.
3 Lana Hask had a sale; Gala shall add half a glass.

down reaches

4 Did my banker, Mr. Mavann, analyze my tax account?
5 Do they, Mr. Zack, expect a number of brave women?
6 Zach, check the menu; next, beckon the lazy valet.

up reaches

7 Prue truly lost the quote we wrote for our report.
8 Teresa quietly put her whole heart into her words.
9 There were two hilarious jokes in your quiet talk.

DRILL 3

Goal: strengthen individual finger reaches

1st finger

1 Bob Mugho hunted for five minutes for your number.
2 Juan hit the bright green turf with his five iron.
3 The frigates and gunboats fought mightily in Java.

2nd finger

4 Dick said the ice on the creek had surely cracked.
5 Even as we picnicked, I decided we needed to diet.
6 Kim, not Mickey, had rice with chicken for dinner.

3rd/4th finger

7 Pam saw Roz wax an aqua auto as Lex sipped a cola.
8 Wally will quickly spell Zeus, Apollo, and Xerxes.
9 Who saw Polly? Zoe Pax saw her; she is quiet now.

DRILL 4

Goal: strengthen special reaches

Emphasize smooth stroking. Avoid pauses, but do not reach for speed.

adjacent reaches

1 Falk knew well that her opinions of art were good.
2 Theresa answered her question; order was restored.
3 We join there and walk north to the western point.

direct reaches

4 Barb Nunn must hunt for my checks; she is in debt.
5 In June and December, Irvin hunts in Bryce Canyon.
6 We decided to carve a number of funny human faces.

double letters

7 Anne stopped off at school to see Bill Wiggs cook.
8 Edd has planned a small cookout for all the troop.
9 Keep adding to my assets all fees that will apply.

| 1 | 2 | 3 | 4 | 5 | 6 | 7 | 8 | 9 | 10 |

Level 2

APPLYING KEYBOARDING SKILL

Learning Outcomes

Numeric Keypad

+ To key the numeric keypad by touch.
+ To develop fluency in using the keypad.

Word Processing Skills

+ To learn and apply basic word processing commands.

Communication Skills

+ To improve basic communication skills.
+ To produce proofreading and editing skills.
+ To compose and edit documents at the keyboard.

Web-Based Computing—Internet, Cloud, and Web 2.0

+ To search for and use Internet information efficiently.
+ To create and send effective e-mails.
+ To explore cloud computing and view and create documents using Web apps.
+ To explore Web 2.0 applications and social media tools.

DRILL 5

Goal: improve troublesome pairs

Use a controlled rate without pauses.

```
     1  ad add did does dish down body dear dread dabs bad
d/k  2  kid ok kiss tuck wick risk rocks kayaks corks buck
     3  Dirk asked Dick to kid Drake about the baked duck.

     4  deed deal den led heed made needs delay he she her
e/i  5  kit kiss kiln kiwi kick kilt kind six ribs kill it
     6  Abie had neither ice cream nor fried rice in Erie.

     7  fib fob fab rib beg bug rob bad bar bed born table
b/v  8  vat vet gave five ever envy never visit weave ever
     9  Did Harv key jibe or jive, TV or TB, robe or rove?

    10  aft after lift gift sit tot the them tax tutu tyro
t/r 11  for far ere era risk rich rock rosy work were roof
    12  In Toronto, Ruth told the truth about her artwork.

    13  jug just jury judge juice unit hunt bonus quiz bug
u/y 14  jay joy lay you your only envy quay oily whey body
    15  Willy usually does not buy your Yukon art in July.
```

DRILL 6

Goal: fluency

```
1  Dian may make cocoa for the girls when they visit.
2  Focus the lens for the right angle; fix the prism.
3  She may suspend work when she signs the torn form.
4  Augment their auto fuel in the keg by the autobus.
5  As usual, their robot did half turns to the right.
6  Pamela laughs as she signals to the big hairy dog.
7  Pay Vivian to fix the island for the eighty ducks.
```

DRILL 7

Goal: eyes on the copy

Option: In the Word Processor, set the Timer for Variable and then either 20" or 30". Choose a *gwam* goal that is two to three words higher than your best rate. Try to reach your goal.

	words 30"	20"
1 Did she make this turkey dish? **ENTER**	12	18
2 Blake and Laurie may go to Dubuque.	14	21
3 Signal for the oak sleigh to turn right.	16	24
4 I blame Susie; did she quench the only flame?	18	27
5 She turns the panel dials to make this robot work.	20	30

LESSON E

KEYBOARDING PRO DELUXE 2 | **Skill Building** | *Accuracy Emphasis*

Select the Skill Building tab; choose the appropriate emphasis and then Lesson E.

KEYBOARDING PRO DELUXE 2 | **Skill Building** | *Technique Builder*

DRILL 14

Word Beginnings

Key each line once, working for accuracy. DS between groups.

br	1	bright brown bramble bread breath breezes brought brother broiler
	2	In February my brother brought brown bread and beans from Boston.
exe	3	exercises exert executives exemplify exemption executed exemplary
	4	They exert extreme effort executing exercises in exemplary style.
bt	5	doubt subtle obtains obtrusion subtracts indebtedness undoubtedly
	6	Extreme debt will cause more than subtle doubt among my creditors.
ny	7	tiny funny company nymph penny nylon many anyone phony any brainy
	8	Anyone as brainy and funny as Penny is an asset to their company.

KEYBOARDING PRO DELUXE 2 | **Timed Writings**

1. Take a 1' writing on each paragraph.
2. Take a 3' writing on both paragraphs.

Writing 27

	gwam 1'	3'
Many people believe that an ounce of prevention is worth a pound	13	4
of cure. Care of your heart can help you prevent serious physical	26	9
problems. The human heart is the most important pump ever	38	13
developed. It constantly pushes blood through the body tissues. But	51	17
the layers of muscle that make up the heart must be kept in proper	65	22
working order. Exercise can help this muscle to remain in good	77	26
condition.	80	27
Another important way of keeping a healthy heart is just to avoid	13	31
habits which are considered detrimental to the body. Food that is high	27	36
in cholesterol is not a good choice. Also, use of tobacco has quite a	41	40
bad effect on the function of the heart. You can minimize your chances	56	45
of heart trouble by avoiding these bad health habits.	66	49

1' | 1 | 2 | 3 | 4 | 5 | 6 | 7 | 8 | 9 | 10 | 11 | 12 | 13
3' | 1 | 2 | 3 | 4

KEYBOARDING PRO DELUXE 2 | **Timed Writings**

Any timed writing in the book can be completed using the Timed Writing feature.

TO USE THE TIMED WRITING FEATURE:

1. Select the Timed Writings tab from the Main screen.
2. Scroll to select the timed writing.
3. Select the source and the timing length. For example,
   - Select Paragraph 1 and 1'. Key paragraph 1; if you finish before time is up, repeat the same paragraph. Always use wordwrap when keying timed writings.
   - Select Paragraph 2 and 1'. Key paragraph 2; repeat the same paragraph if you finish before time is up.
   - Select the Entire Writing and 2'. Try to maintain your 1' rate. If you finish before time is up, start over, beginning with paragraph 1.
4. Timings save automatically.
5. The Timed Writing Report displays the results of the last 40 timed writings and the best 3 timings at each speed.

wordwrap

E **ALL LETTERS**

Goal: build staying power

1. Key each paragraph as a 1' timing. **Use wordwrap.**
2. Key a 2' timing on both paragraphs. **Use wordwrap.**

gwam 2'

Writing 1: **18 *gwam***

Why spend weeks with some problem when just a few quiet 6
minutes can help us to resolve it. 9
If we don't take time to think through a problem, it will 15
swiftly begin to expand in size. 18

Writing 2: **20 *gwam***

We push very hard in our quest for growth, and we all 5
think that only excellent growth will pay off. 10
Believe it or not, one can actually work much too hard, 16
be much too zealous, and just miss the mark. 20

Writing 3: **22 *gwam***

A business friend once explained to me why he was often 6
quite eager to be given some new project to work with. 11
My friend said that each new project means he has to 16
organize and use the best of his knowledge and his skill. 22

Writing 4: **24 *gwam***

Don't let new words get away from you. Learn how to spell 6
and pronounce new words and when and how finally to use them. 12
A new word is a friend, but frequently more. New words 18
must be used lavishly to extend the size of your own word power. 24

2' | 1 | 2 | 3 | 4 | 5 | 6 |

LESSON D

KEYBOARDING PRO DELUXE 2 | **Skill Building** | *Accuracy Emphasis*

Select the Skill Building tab; choose the appropriate emphasis and then Lesson D.

KEYBOARDING PRO DELUXE 2 | **Skill Building** | *Technique Builder*

DRILL 13

Adjacent Key Review

Key each line once; strive for accuracy. DS between groups.

1 nm many enmity solemn kl inkling weekly pickle oi oil invoice join
2 iu stadium medium genius lk milk talk walks uy buy buyer soliloquy
3 mn alumni hymn number column sd Thursday wisdom df mindful handful
4 me mention comment same fo found perform info le letter flew files

5 The buyer sent his weekly invoices for oil to the group on Thursday.
6 Mindful of the alumni, the choirs sang a hymn prior to my soliloquy.
7 An inmate, a fogger, and a genius joined the weekly talks on Monday.
8 They were to join in the talk shows to assess regions of the Yukon.

KEYBOARDING PRO DELUXE 2 | **Timed Writings**

1. Take a 1' writing on each paragraph.
2. Take a 3' writing on both paragraphs.

Writing 26

	gwam 1'	3'
All people, in spite of their eating habits, have two major needs	13	4
that must be met by their food. They need food that provides a	26	9
source of energy, and they need food that will fill the skeletal and	40	13
operating needs of their bodies. Carbohydrates, fats, and protein	53	18
form a major portion of the diet. Vitamins and minerals are also	66	22
necessary for excellent health.	72	24
Carbohydrates make up a major source of our energy needs.	12	28
Fats also serve as a source of energy and act as defense against	25	32
cold and trauma. Proteins are changed to amino acids, which are	38	37
the building units of the body. These, in turn, are utilized to make	52	41
most body tissue. Minerals are required to control many body	64	45
functions, and vitamins are used for normal growth and aid against	77	50
disease.	84	52

1' | 1 | 2 | 3 | 4 | 5 | 6 | 7 | 8 | 9 | 10 | 11 | 12 | 13 |
3' | 1 | 2 | 3 | 4 |

Note: The dot above text represents two words.

Writing 5: 26 *gwam* *gwam* 2'

We usually get best results when we know where we are 5
going. Just setting a few goals will help us quietly see what 12
we are doing. 13

Goals can help measure whether we are moving at a good 19
rate or dozing along. You can expect a goal to help you find 25
good results. 26

Writing 6: 28 *gwam*

To win whatever prizes we want from life, we must plan to 6
move carefully from this goal to the next to get the maximum 12
result from our work. 14

If we really want to become skilled in keying, we must 19
come to see that this desire will require of us just a little 26
patience and hard work. 28

Writing 7: 30 *gwam*

Am I an individual person? I'm sure I am; still, in a 5
much, much bigger sense, other people have a major voice in 12
thoughts I think and actions I take. 15

Although we are each a unique person, we all work and 21
play in organized groups of people who do not expect us to 26
dismiss their rules of law and order. 30

2' | 1 | 2 | 3 | 4 | 5 | 6 |

LESSON C

KEYBOARDING PRO DELUXE 2 | **Skill Building** | *Accuracy Emphasis*

Select the Skill Building tab, the appropriate emphasis, and then Lesson C. Your results will be summarized in the Skill Building Report.

KEYBOARDING PRO DELUXE 2 | **Skill Building** | *Technique Builder*

DRILL 12

Balanced-Hand

Key each line once for fluency; DS between groups.

1 an anyone brand spans th their father eighth he head sheets niche
2 en enters depends been nd end handle fund or original sport color
3 ur urban turns assure to took factory photo ti titles satin still
4 ic ice bicycle chic it item position profit ng angle danger doing

5 I want the info in the file on the profits from the chic bicycle.
6 The original of the color photo she took of the factory is there.
7 Assure them that anyone can turn onto the road to the urban area.
8 The color of the title sheet depends on the photos and the funds.

KEYBOARDING PRO DELUXE 2 | **Timed Writings**

1. Take a 1' writing on each paragraph.
2. Take a 3' writing on both paragraphs.

Writing 25

Text	gwam 1'	3'
Practicing basic health rules will result in good body condition.	14	5
Proper diet is a way to achieve good health. Eat a variety of foods each	28	9
day, including some fruit, vegetables, cereal products, and foods rich	42	14
in protein, to be sure that you keep a balance. Another part of a good	57	19
health plan is physical activity, such as running.	67	22
Running has become popular in this country. A long run is a big	13	27
challenge to many males and females to determine just how far they	26	31
can go in a given time, or the time they require to cover a measured	40	36
distance. Long runs of fifty or one hundred miles are on measured	53	40
courses with refreshments available every few miles. Daily training is	67	45
necessary in order to maximize endurance.	76	48

1' | 1 | 2 | 3 | 4 | 5 | 6 | 7 | 8 | 9 | 10 | 11 | 12 | 13 |
3' | 1 | 2 | 3 | 4 |

MODULE 2

Figure and Symbol Keys

Lessons 14–18	*Figure Keys*
Lessons 19–24	*Symbol Keys*
Lessons 25	*Assessment*

LEARNING OUTCOMES

- Key the numeric keys by touch.
- Use symbol keys correctly.
- Build keying speed and accuracy.
- Apply correct number expression.
- Apply proofreaders' marks.

Lesson 14 | *1 and 8*

WARMUP

KEYBOARDING PRO DELUXE 2

Lessons/14a Warmup

Key each line twice.

Line 2: Space once after a series of brief questions within a sentence.

alphabet 1 Jessie Quick believed the campaign frenzy would be exciting.

space bar 2 Was it Mary? Helen? Pam? It was a woman; I saw one of them.

3rd row 3 We were quietly prepped to write two letters to Portia York.

easy 4 Kale's neighbor works with a tutor when they visit downtown.

| 1 | 2 | 3 | 4 | 5 | 6 | 7 | 8 | 9 | 10 | 11 | 12 |

Skill Building

14b Textbook Keying

The words at the right are from the 100 most used words.

Key each line once; work for fluency.

Top 100 High-Frequency Words

5 a an it been copy for his this more no office please service

6 our service than the they up was work all any many thank had

7 business from I know made more not me new of some to program

8 such these two with your about and have like department year

9 by at on but do had in letter most now one please you should

10 their order like also appreciate that there gentlemen letter

11 be can each had information letter may make now only so that

12 them time use which am other been send to enclosed have will

LESSON B

KEYBOARDING PRO DELUXE 2 | **Skill Building** | *Accuracy Emphasis*

1. Select the Skill Building tab and choose either Speed Emphasis or Accuracy Emphasis as recommended in Assessment 1. Complete Lesson B.
2. Your results will be summarized in the Skill Building Report.

KEYBOARDING PRO DELUXE 2 | **Skill Building** | *Technique Builder*

DRILL 11

Balanced-Hand Combinations

Key each line once, working for fluency. DS between groups.

1 to today stocks into ti times sitting until ur urges further tour
2 en entire trend dozen or order support editor nd and mandate land
3 he healthy check ache th these brother both an annual change plan
4 nt into continue want of office softer roof is issue poison basis

5 My brother urged the editor to have an annual health check today.
6 The manager will support the change to order our stock annually.
7 The time for the land tour will not change until further notice.
8 Did the letter mention her position or performance in the office?

KEYBOARDING PRO DELUXE 2 | **Timed Writings**

1. Key a 1' writing on each paragraph. Compare your *gwam*.
2. Key additional 1' writings on the slower paragraph.

Writing 24

gwam 1' | 3'

Most of us, at some time, have had a valid reason to complain— 12 | 6
about a defective product, poor service, or perhaps being tired of 26 | 13
talking to voice mail. Many of us feel that complaining, however, 39 | 20
to a firm is an exercise in futility and don't bother to express 52 | 26
our dissatisfaction. We just write it off to experience and 64 | 32
continue to be ripped off. 70 | 35

Today, more than at anytime in the past consumers are taking some 12 | 6
steps to let their feelings be known—and with a great amount of 25 | 13
success. As a result, firms are becoming more responsive to 38 | 19
the needs of the consumer. complaints from customers alert firms 51 | 26
to produce or service defect and there by cause action to be taken 65 | 33
for their benefit. 70 | 35

1' | 1 | 2 | 3 | 4 | 5 | 6 | 7 | 8 | 9 | 10 | 11 | 12 | 13
3' | 1 | 2 | 3 | 4

New Keys

14c 1 and 8

Key each line once.

Note: The digit "1" and the letter "l" have separate values on a computer keyboard. Do not interchange these characters.

Abbreviations: Do not space after a period within an abbreviation, as in Ph.D., U.S., C.O.D., a.m.

1 Reach *up* with *left fourth* finger.

8 Reach *up* with *right second* finger.

1

13 1 la al 1 1; 1 and a 1; 1 add 1; 1 aunt; 1 ace; 1 arm; 1 aye
14 1 and 11 and 111; 11 eggs; 11 vats; Set 11A; May 11; Item 11
15 The 11 aces of the 111th Corps each rated a salute at 1 p.m.

8

16 8 8k k8 8 8; 8 kits; ask 8; 8 kites; kick 8; 8 keys; spark 8
17 OK 88; 8 bags; 8 or 88; the 88th; 88 kegs; ask 88; order 888
18 Eight of the 88 cars score 8 or better on our Form 8 rating.

all figures learned

19 She did live at 818 Park, not 181 Park; or was it 181 Clark?
20 Put 1 with 8 to form 18; put 8 with 1 to form 81. Use 1881.
21 On May 1 at 8 a.m., 18 men and 18 women left Gate 8 for Rio.

Skill Building

14d Reinforcement

Key each line. Key with accuracy.

figures

22 Our 188 trucks moved 1881 tons on August 18 and December 18.
23 Send Mary 181 No. 188 panes for her home at 8118 Oak Street.
24 The 188 men in 8 boats left Docks 1 and 18 at 1 p.m., May 1.

25 pop was lap pass slaw wool solo swap Apollo wasp load plaque
26 Was Polly acquainted with the skillful jazz player in Texas?
27 The computer is a useful tool; it helps you to perform well.

14e Speed Builder

Key these lines in the game.

28 Did their form entitle them to the land?
29 Did the men in the field signal for us to go?
30 I may pay for the antique bowls when I go to town.
31 The auditor did the work right, so he risks no penalty.
32 The man by the big bush did signal us to turn down the lane.

| 1 | 2 | 3 | 4 | 5 | 6 | 7 | 8 | 9 | 10 | 11 | 12 |

Skill Builder 3

LESSON A

KEYBOARDING PRO DELUXE 2 **Skill Building** *Accuracy Emphasis*

1. Select the Skill Building tab, Accuracy Emphasis, and then Assessment 1.

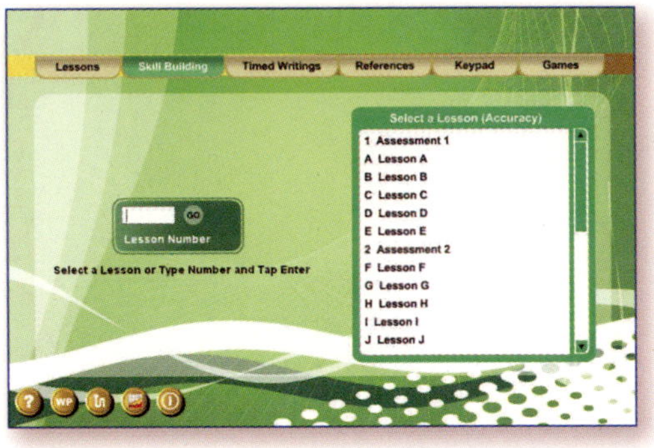

2. Key the timing from the screen for 3'; work for control.
3. Complete Lesson A or the first lesson you have not completed in either Speed Emphasis or Accuracy Emphasis as suggested by the software.
4. Your results will be summarized in the Skill Building Report.

KEYBOARDING PRO DELUXE 2 **Timed Writings**

Writing 23

1. Key a 1' writing on each paragraph. (Remember to change the source in the Timed Writing Settings dialog box.) Compare your *gwam* on the two paragraphs.
2. Key additional 1' writings on the slower paragraph.

	gwam 1'	3'
There are many qualities which cause good employees to stand	12	6
out in a group. In the first place, they keep their minds on the	25	13
task at hand. Also, they often think about the work they do and	38	19
how it relates to the total efforts of the project. They keep	52	26
their eyes, ears, and minds open to new ideas.	60	30
Second, good workers may be classed as those who work at a	13	6
steady pace. Far too many people work by bits and pieces. They	25	13
begin one thing, but then they allow themselves to be easily taken	39	19
away from the work at hand. A lot of people are good starters,	52	26
but many less of them are also good finishers.	60	30

1' | 1 | 2 | 3 | 4 | 5 | 6 | 7 | 8 | 9 | 10 | 11 | 12 | 13 |
3' | 1 | 2 | 3 | 4 |

Lesson 15 | 5 and 0

WARMUP

KEYBOARDING PRO DELUXE 2

Lessons/15a Warmup

Key each line twice.

For a series of capital letters, tap CAPS LOCK with the left little finger. Tap again to release.

alphabet 1 John Quigley packed the zinnias in twelve large, firm boxes.

1/8 2 Idle Motor 18 at 8 mph and Motor 81 at 8 mph; avoid Motor 1.

caps 3 Lily read BLITHE SPIRIT by Noel Coward. I read VANITY FAIR.

lock 4 Did they fix the problem of the torn panel and worn element?

| 1 | 2 | 3 | 4 | 5 | 6 | 7 | 8 | 9 | 10 | 11 | 12 |

15b Technique Reinforcement

Reach up or down without moving your hands. Key each line once; repeat drill.

adjacent reaches

5 as oil red ask wet opt mop try tree open shred operas treaty

6 were pore dirt stew ruin faster onion alumni dreary mnemonic

7 The opened red hydrants were powerful, fast, and very dirty.

outside reaches

8 pop zap cap zag wasp equip lazy zippers queue opinion quartz

9 zest waste paper exist parquet azalea acquaint apollo apathy

10 The lazy wasp passed the potted azalea on the parquet floor.

New Keys

15c 5 and 0

Key each line once.

5 Reach *up* with *left first* finger.

0 Reach *up* with *right fourth* finger.

5

11 5 5f f5 5 5; 5 fans; 5 feet; 5 figs; 5 fobs; 5 furs; 5 flaws

12 5 o'clock; 5 a.m.; 5 p.m.; is 55 or less; buy 55; 5 and 5 is

13 Call Line 555 if 5 fans or 5 bins arrive at Pier 5 by 5 p.m.

0

14 0 0; ;0 0 0; skip 0; plan 0; left 0; is below 0; I scored 0;

15 0 degrees; key 0 and 0; write 00 here; the total is 0 or 00;

16 She laughed at their 0 to 0 score; but ours was 0 to 0 also.

all figures learned

17 I keyed 550 pages for Invoice 05, or 50 more than we needed.

18 Pages 15 and 18 of the program listed 150, not 180, members.

19 On May 10, Rick drove 500 miles to New Mexico in car No. 08.

Writing 20

3' | 5'

If asked, most people will agree that some people have far 4 | 2 | 21
more creative skills than others, and they will also say that 8 | 5 | 34
these skills are in great demand by most organizations. A follow- 12 | 7 | 37
up question is in order. Are you born with creative skills or 17 | 10 | 39
can you develop them? No easy answer to that question exists, but 21 | 13 | 42
it is worth spending a bit of time pondering. 24 | 15 | 44

If creative skills can be developed, then the next issue is 28 | 17 | 46
how can you develop these skills. One way is to approach each 32 | 19 | 49
task with a determination to solve the problem and a refusal to 37 | 22 | 51
accept failure. If the normal way of doing a job does not work, 41 | 25 | 54
just keep trying things never tried before until you reach a good 45 | 27 | 56
solution. This is called thinking outside the box. 49 | 29 | 58

3' | 1 | 2 | 3 | 4
5' | 1 | 2 | 3

Writing 21

1' | 3'

Figures are not as easy to key as many of the words we use. 12 | 4 | 36
Balanced-hand figures such as 16, 27, 38, 49, and 50, although 25 | 8 | 40
fairly easy, are slower to key because each one requires longer 37 | 12 | 44
reaches and uses more time per stroke. 45 | 16 | 46

Figures such as 12, 45, 67, and 90 are even more difficult 12 | 20 | 50
because they are next to one another and each uses just a single 25 | 25 | 54
hand to key. Because of their size, bigger numbers such as 178, 39 | 29 | 59
349, and 1,220 create extra speed losses. 45 | 32 | 61

1' | 1 | 2 | 3 | 4 | 5 | 6 | 7 | 8 | 9 | 10 | 11 | 12 | 13
3' | 1 | 2 | 3 | 4

Writing 22

1' | 2'

Few people attain financial success without some kind of 11 | 6
planning. People who realize the value of prudent spending and 24 | 12
saving are those who set up a budget. A budget helps individ- 36 | 18
uals determine just how much they can spend and how much they 49 | 24
can save so that they will not squander their money recklessly. 61 | 31

Keeping records is a ~~crucial~~ *vital* part of ~~a~~ budget*ing*. ~~Complete~~ *A detailed* 12 | 6
record~~s~~ of *all* income and expen~~ses~~*ditures* over a period of ~~a number of~~ *several* 24 | 12
months ~~can~~ *will* help ~~to~~ determine what bills, ~~as water~~ *like utilities* or rent, are 37 | 18
~~static~~ *fixed* and which are flexible. To get the most out of your 49 | 25
income, ~~pay~~ *focus* attention ~~to~~ *on* the items that ~~you~~ can ~~modify~~ *be changed*. 61 | 30

1' | 1 | 2 | 3 | 4 | 5 | 6 | 7 | 8 | 9 | 10 | 11 | 12
2' | 1 | 2 | 3 | 4 | 5 | 6

Skill Transfer

1. Set the Timer for 2'. Take a 2' writing on paragraph 1.
2. Set the Timer for 2'. Take a 2' writing on paragraph 2.
3. Take 2 or more 2' writings on the slower paragraph.

Skill Building

15d Textbook Keying

Key each line once; DS between 3-line groups.

improve figures

20 Read pages 5 and 8; duplicate page 18; omit pages 50 and 51.
21 We have Model 80 with 10 meters or Model 180 with 15 meters.
22 After May 18, French 050 meets in room 15 at 10 a.m. daily.

improve long reaches

23 Barb Abver saw a vibrant version of her brave venture on TV.
24 Call a woman or a man who will manage Minerva Manor in Nome.
25 We were quick to squirt a quantity of water at Quin and West.

15e Timed Writing

Take a 2' writing on both paragraphs. End the lesson; go to the Word Processor to complete 15e. **Use wordwrap.**

E ALL LETTERS

	gwam 2'	3'
I thought about Harry and how he had worked for me for	6	4
10 years; how daily at 8 he parked his worn car in the lot;	12	8
then, he left at 5. Every day was almost identical for him.	18	12
In a quiet way, he did his job well, asking for little	23	15
attention. So I never recognized his thirst for travel. I	29	19
didn't expect to find all of those maps near his workplace.	35	23

2' | 1 | 2 | 3 | 4 | 5 | 6 |
3' | 1 | 2 | 3 | 4 |

15f Tab Review

1. Read the instructions to clear and set tabs.
2. Go to the Word Processor. Set a left tab at 4".
3. Practice the lines; tap TAB without watching your keyboard.

STANDARD PLAN for Setting and Clearing Tabs in the Word Processor

Preset or default tabs are displayed on the Ruler. If necessary, display the Ruler in the Word Processor. (Choose Horizontal Ruler on the View menu.) Sometimes you will want to remove or clear existing tabs before setting new ones.

To clear and set tabs:

1. On the menu bar, click Format, and then Clear All Tabs.
2. To set tabs: From the Format menu, select Set Tab. Select the type of tab you want to set (left, center, decimal, or right); enter the position and click OK.

Option: Click the left or right mouse button directly on the Ruler to set either a left or right tab.

		Set tab 4"
	→ Tab	Keyboarding
has become	→ Tab	the primary
means of	→ Tab	written communication
in business and	→ Tab	in our personal lives.
Keyboarding is	→ Tab	used by persons
in every profession	→ Tab	and most job levels.

Writing 17

Text	gwam 1'	3'	
Many people like to say just how lucky a person is when	11	4	29
he or she succeeds in doing something well. Does luck play a	24	8	33
large role in success? In some cases, it might have a small	36	12	37
effect.	37	13	38
Being in the right place at the right time may help, but	11	16	41
hard work may help far more than luck. Those who just wait for	24	20	46
luck should not expect quick results and should realize luck	36	24	50
may never come.	39	26	51

1' | 1 | 2 | 3 | 4 | 5 | 6 | 7 | 8 | 9 | 10 | 11 | 12
3' | 1 | 2 | 3 | 4

Writing 18

Text	gwam 1'	3'	
New golfers must learn to zero in on just a few social	11	4	39
rules. Do not talk, stand close, or move around when another	23	8	44
person is hitting. Be ready to play when it is your turn.	35	12	47
Take practice swings in an area away from other people.	11	15	51
Let the group behind you play through if your group is slow.	24	20	55
Do not rest on your club on the green when waiting your turn.	36	23	59
Set your other clubs down off the green. Leave the green	12	27	63
quickly when done; update your card on the next tee. Be sure	24	31	67
to leave the course in good condition. Always have a good time.	37	36	72

1' | 1 | 2 | 3 | 4 | 5 | 6 | 7 | 8 | 9 | 10 | 11 | 12
3' | 1 | 2 | 3 | 4

Writing 19

Text	gwam 1'	3'	
Do you know how to use time wisely? If you do, then its	11	4	51
proper use can help you organize and run a business better.	24	8	55
If you find that your daily problems tend to keep you from	35	12	59
planning properly, then perhaps you are not using time well.	48	16	63
You may find that you spend too much time on tasks that are	60	20	67
not important. Plan your work to save valuable time.	70	24	70
A firm that does not plan is liable to run into trouble.	12	27	74
A small firm may have trouble planning. It is important	23	31	78
to know just where the firm is headed. A firm may have a	35	35	82
fear of learning things it would rather not know. To say	46	39	86
that planning is easy would be absurd. It requires lots of	58	43	90
thinking and planning to meet the expected needs of the firm.	70	47	94

1' | 1 | 2 | 3 | 4 | 5 | 6 | 7 | 8 | 9 | 10 | 11 | 12
3' | 1 | 2 | 3 | 4

Lesson 16 | *2 and 7*

WARMUP

KEYBOARDING PRO DELUXE 2 — *Lessons/16a Warmup*

Key each line twice.

alphabet 1 Perry might know I feel jinxed because I have missed a quiz.
figures 2 Channels 5 and 8, on from 10 to 11, said Luisa's IQ was 150.
caps lock 3 Ella Hill will see Chekhov's THE CHERRY ORCHARD on Czech TV.
easy 4 The big dog by the bush kept the ducks and hen in the field.

| 1 | 2 | 3 | 4 | 5 | 6 | 7 | 8 | 9 | 10 | 11 | 12 |

New Keys

16b 2 and 7

Key each line once.

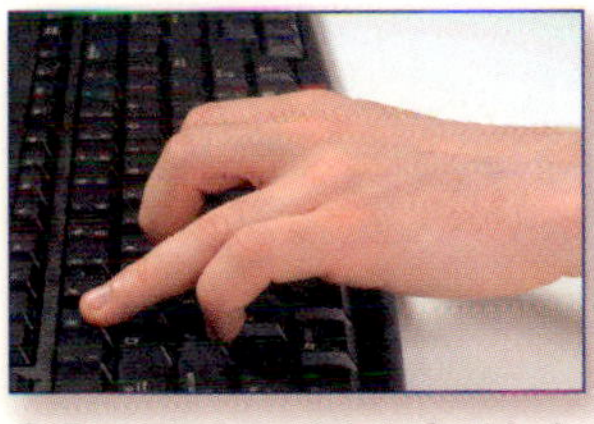

2 Reach *up* with *left third* finger.

7 Reach *up* with *right first* finger.

2

5 2 2s s2 2 2; has 2 sons; is 2 sizes; was 2 sites; has 2 skis
6 add 2 and 2; 2 sets of 2; catch 22; as 2 of the 22; 222 Main
7 Exactly at 2 on April 22, the 22nd Company left from Pier 2.

7

8 7 7j j7 7 7; 7 jets; 7 jeans; 7 jays; 7 jobs; 7 jars; 7 jaws
9 ask for 7; buy 7; 77 years; June 7; take any 7; deny 77 boys
10 From May 7 on, all 77 men will live at 777 East 77th Street.

all figures learned

11 I read 2 of the 72 books, Ellis read 7, and Han read all 72.
12 Tract 27 cites the date as 1850; Tract 170 says it was 1852.
13 You can take Flight 850 on January 12; I'll take Flight 705.

16c Number Reinforcement

Key each line. Concentrate as you reach to the top row.

8/1 14 line 8; Book 1; No. 88; Seat 11; June 18; Cart 81; date 1881
2/7 15 take 2; July 7; buy 22; sell 77; mark 27; adds 72; Memo 2772
5/0 16 feed 5; bats 0; age 50; Ext. 55; File 50; 55 bags; band 5005
all 17 I work 18 visual signs with 20 turns of the 57 lenses to 70.
all 18 Did 17 boys fix the gears for 50 bicycles in 28 racks or 10?

Writing 14

gwam 1' | 3'

What do you expect when you travel to a foreign country? 12 4
Quite a few people realize that one of the real joys of 23 8
traveling is to get a brief glimpse of how others think, work, 36 12
and live. 40 12
The best way to enjoy a different culture is to learn as 11 16
much about it as you can before you leave home. Then you can 24 20
concentrate on being a good guest rather than trying to find 36 24
local people who can meet your needs. 44 27

Writing 15

gwam 1' | 3'

What do you enjoy doing in your free time? Health experts 12 4
tell us that far too many people choose to be lazy rather than 24 8
to be active. The result of that decision shows up in our 36 12
weight. 37 13
Working to control what we weigh is not easy, and seldom 12 16
can it be done quickly. However, it is quite important if our 24 21
weight exceeds what it should be. Part of the problem results 37 25
from the amount and type of food we eat. 44 27
If we want to look fit, we should include exercise as a 11 31
substantial part of our weight loss plan. Walking at least 23 35
thirty minutes each day at a very fast rate can make a big 35 39
difference both in our appearance and in the way we feel. 47 42

Writing 16

gwam 1' | 3'

Doing what we like to do is quite important; however, 10 4
liking what we have to do is equally important. As you ponder 23 8
both of these concepts, you may feel that they are the same, 36 12
but they are not the same. 41 14
If we could do only those things that we prefer to do, the 12 18
chances are that we would do them exceptionally well. Generally, 25 22
we will take more pride in doing those things we like doing, 37 26
and we will not quit until we get them done right. 47 29
We realize, though, that we cannot restrict the things 11 33
that we must do just to those that we want to do. Therefore, 23 37
we need to build an interest in and an appreciation of all the 36 41
tasks that we must do in our positions. 44 44

1'	1	2	3	4	5	6	7	8	9	10	11	12
3'		1			2			3			4	

Skill Building

16d Textbook Keying

Key each line once to review reaches; fingers curved and relaxed; wrists low. DS between groups.

3rd/4th
19 pop was lap pass slaw wool solo swap apollo wasp load plaque
20 Al's quote was, "I was dazzled by the jazz, pizza, and pool."

1st/2nd
21 bad fun nut kick dried night brick civic thick hutch believe
22 Kim may visit her friends in Germany if I give her a ticket.

3rd/1st
23 cry tube wine quit very curb exit crime ebony mention excite
24 To be invited, petition the six executive committee members.

16e Textbook Keying

Key each line once; DS between 3-line groups. Do not pause at the end of lines.

TECHNIQUE TIP

Think and key the words and phrases as units rather than letter by letter.

words: *think, say,* and *key* words

25 is do am lay cut pen dub may fob ale rap cot hay pay hem box
26 box wit man sir fish also hair giant rigor civic virus ivory
27 laugh sight flame audit formal social turkey bicycle problem

phrases: *think, say,* and *key* phrases

28 is it | is it | if it is | if it is | or by | or by | or me | or me | for us
29 and all | for pay | pay dues and | the pen | the pen box | the pen box
30 such forms | held both | work form | then wish | sign name | with them

easy sentences

31 The man is to do the work right; he then pays the neighbors.
32 Sign the forms to pay the eight men for the turkey and hams.
33 The antique ivory bicycle is a social problem for the chair.

| 1 | 2 | 3 | 4 | 5 | 6 | 7 | 8 | 9 | 10 | 11 | 12 |

16f Timed Writing

Take a 2' timing on both paragraphs. Repeat the timing. **Use wordwrap.**

gwam 2' | 3'

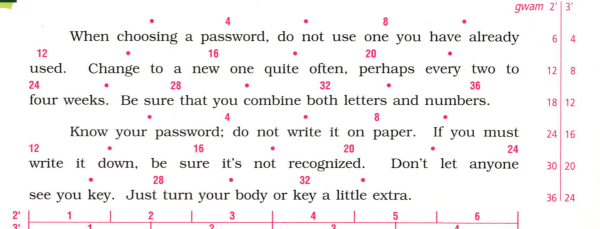

When choosing a password, do not use one you have already 6 | 4
used. Change to a new one quite often, perhaps every two to 12 | 8
four weeks. Be sure that you combine both letters and numbers. 18 | 12

Know your password; do not write it on paper. If you must 24 | 16
write it down, be sure it's not recognized. Don't let anyone 30 | 20
see you key. Just turn your body or key a little extra. 36 | 24

2' | 1 | 2 | 3 | 4 | 5 | 6 |
3' | 1 | 2 | 3 | 4 |

Writing 11

gwam 3'

Anyone who expects some day to find an excellent job should 4 | 34
begin now to learn the value of accuracy. To be worth anything, 8 | 38
completed work must be correct, without question. Naturally, we 13 | 43
realize that the human aspect of the work equation always raises 17 | 47
the prospect of errors; but we should understand that those same 20 | 51
errors can be found and fixed. Every completed job should carry 26 | 56
at least one stamp; the stamp of pride in work that is exemplary. 30 | 60

Writing 12

No question about it: Many personal problems we face today 4 | 34
arise from the fact that we earthlings have never been very wise 8 | 38
consumers. We haven't consumed our natural resources well; as a 13 | 43
result, we have jeopardized much of our environment. We excused 17 | 47
our behavior because we thought that our stock of most resources 20 | 51
had no limit. So, finally, we are beginning to realize just how 26 | 56
indiscreet we were; and we are taking steps to rebuild our world. 30 | 60

Writing 13

When I see people in top jobs, I know I'm seeing people who 4 | 34
sell. I'm not just referring to employees who labor in a retail 8 | 38
outlet; I mean those people who put extra effort into convincing 13 | 43
others to recognize their best qualities. They, themselves, are 17 | 47
the commodity they sell; and their optimum tools are appearance, 20 | 51
language, and personality. They look great, they talk and write 26 | 56
well; and, with candid self-confidence, they meet you eye to eye. 30 | 60

3' | 1 | 2 | 3 | 4

Lesson 17 | 4 and 9

KEYBOARDING PRO DELUXE 2

WARMUP

Warmup 17a

Key each line twice.

alphabet 1 Bob realized very quickly that jumping was excellent for us.
figures 2 Has each of the 18 clerks now corrected Item 501 on page 27?
shift keys 3 L. K. Coe, M.D., hopes Dr. Lopez can leave for Maine in May.
easy 4 The men paid their own firms for the eight big enamel signs.

New Keys

17b 4 and 9

Key each line once.

4 Reach *up* with *left first* finger.

9 Reach *up* with *right third* finger.

4

5 4 4f f4 4 4 4; if 4 furs; off 4 floors; gaff 4 fish; 4 flags
6 44th floor; half of 44; 4 walked 44 flights; 4 girls; 4 boys
7 I order exactly 44 bagels, 4 cakes, and 4 pies before 4 a.m.

9

8 9 9l l9 9 9 9; fill 9 lugs; call 9 lads; Bill 9 lost; dial 9
9 also 9 oaks; roll 9 loaves; 9.9 degrees; sell 9 oaks; Hall 9
10 Just 9 couples, 9 men and 9 women, left at 9 on our Tour 99.

all figures learned

11 Memo 94 says 9 pads, 4 pens, and 4 ribbons were sent July 9.
12 Study Item 17 and Item 28 on page 40 and Item 59 on page 49.
13 Within 17 months he drove 85 miles, walked 29, and flew 490.

Skill Building

17c Textbook Keying

Key each line once.

14 My staff of 18 worked 11 hours a day from May 27 to June 12.
15 There were 5 items tested by Inspector 7 at 4 p.m. on May 8.
16 Please send her File 10 today at 8; her access number is 97.
17 Car 47 had its trial run. The qualifying speed was 198 mph.
18 The estimated score? 485. Actual? 190. Difference? 295.

Assess skill growth:

1. Select the Timed Writings tab from the Main menu.

   Timed Writings

2. Select the writing number such as Writing 8.
3. Select 3' as the length of the writing. **Use wordwrap.**
4. Repeat the timing if desired.

Word Processor option:

1. Key 1' writings on each paragraph of a timing. Note that paragraphs within a timing increase by two words. **Goal:** to complete each paragraph
2. Key a 3' timing on the entire writing.

gwam 1' | 3'

Writing 8

Any of us whose target is to achieve success in our professional 13 4
lives will understand that we must learn how to work in harmony 26 8
with others whose paths may cross ours daily. 35 12

We will, unquestionably, work for, with, and beside people, just 13 16
as they will work for, with, and beside us. We will judge them, 26 20
as most certainly they are going to be judging us. 38 24

A lot of people realize the need for solid working relations and 13 28
have a rule that treats others as they, themselves, expect to be 26 33
treated. This seems to be a sound, practical idea for them. 40 37

Writing 9

I spoke with one company visitor recently; and she was very much 13 4
impressed, she said, with the large amount of work she had noted 26 9
being finished by one of our front office workers. 36 12

I told her how we had just last week recognized this very person 13 16
for what he had done, for output, naturally, but also because of 26 21
its excellence. We know this person has that "magic touch." 38 25

This "magic touch" is the ability to do a fair amount of work in 13 29
a fair amount of time. It involves a desire to become ever more 26 34
efficient without losing quality--the "touch" all workers should 39 38
have. 40 38

Writing 10

Isn't it great just to untangle and relax after you have keyed a 13 4
completed document? Complete, or just done? No document is 25 8
quite complete until it has left you and passed to the next step. 38 13

There are desirable things that must happen to a document before 13 17
you surrender it. It must be read carefully, first of all, for 26 22
meaning to find words that look right but aren't. Read word for 39 26
word. 40 26

Check all figures and exact data, like a date or time, with your 13 31
principal copy. Make sure format details are right. Only then, 26 35
print or remove the work and scrutinize to see how it might look 39 39
to a recipient. 42 40

1' | 1 | 2 | 3 | 4 | 5 | 6 | 7 | 8 | 9 | 10 | 11 | 12 | 13
3' | 1 | 2 | 3 | 4

17d Technique Reinforcement

Key smoothly; tap the keys at a brisk, steady pace.

first finger

19 buy them gray vent guy brunt buy brunch much give huge vying
20 Hagen, after her July triumph at tennis, may try volleyball.
21 Verna urges us to buy yet another of her beautiful rag rugs.

second finger

22 keen idea; kick it back; ice breaker; decide the issue; cite
23 Did Dick ask Cecelia, his sister, if she decided to like me?
24 Suddenly, Micki's bike skidded on the Cedar Street ice rink.

third/fourth finger

25 low slow lax solo wax zip zap quips quiz zipper prior icicle
26 Paula has always allowed us to relax at La Paz and at Quito.
27 Please ask Zale to explain who explores most aquatic slopes.

17e Timed Writing

Take a 2' timing on both paragraphs. Repeat the timing. **Use wordwrap.**

E ALL LETTERS

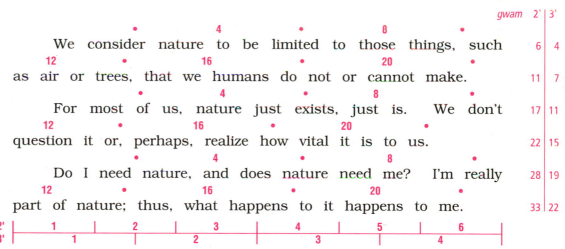

	gwam 2'	3'
We consider nature to be limited to those things, such	6	4
as air or trees, that we humans do not or cannot make.	11	7
For most of us, nature just exists, just is. We don't	17	11
question it or, perhaps, realize how vital it is to us.	22	15
Do I need nature, and does nature need me? I'm really	28	19
part of nature; thus, what happens to it happens to me.	33	22

2' | 1 | 2 | 3 | 4 | 5 | 6
3' | 1 | 2 | 3 | 4

17f Enrichment

1. Click the Skill Building tab from the main menu and choose Technique Builder; select Drill 2.
2. Key Drill 2 from page 32. Key each line once striving for good accuracy.
3. The results will be listed on the Skill Building Report.

TECHNIQUE TIP

Keep hands quiet and fingers well curved over the keys. Do not allow your fingers to bounce.

Skill Builder 2

KEYBOARDING PRO DELUXE 2 | **Skill Building** | *Technique Builder*

Select the Skill Building tab from the Main menu and then Technique Builder. Select the drill and follow the directions in the book.

DRILL 8

Opposite Hand Reaches

Key each line once and DS between groups of lines. Key at a controlled rate; concentrate on the reaches.

i/e

1 ik is fit it sit laid site like insist still wise coil light
2 ed he ear the fed egg led elf lake jade heat feet hear where
3 lie kite item five aide either quite linear imagine brighter
4 Imagine the aide eating the pears before the grieving tiger.

w/o

5 ws we way was few went wit law with weed were week gnaw when
6 ol on go hot old lot joy odd comb open tool upon money union
7 bow owl word wood worm worse tower brown toward wrote weapon
8 The workers lowered the brown swords toward the wood weapon.

DRILL 9

Proofreaders' Marks

Key each line once and DS after each sentence. Correct the sentence as edited, making all handwritten corrections. Do not key the numbers.

- Capitalize
- Change letter
- Close up space
- Delete
- Insert
- Lowercase
- Space
- Transpose

1. When a writer create the preliminary version of a document, they are concentrating on conveying the intended ideas.
2. This ver sion of a preleminary document is called a rough.
3. After the draft is created the Writer edits refines the copy.
4. Sometimes proofreader's marks are used to edit the draft.
5. The changes will them be make to the original.
6. After the changes have been made, then the Writer reads the copy.
7. Edit ing and proofreading requires alot of time and effort.
8. An attitute of excellance is reqiured to produce error free message.

DRILL 10

Proofreading

Compare your sentences in Drill 9 with Drill 10. How did you do? Now key the paragraph for fluency. Concentrate on keying as accurately as possible.

When a writer creates the preliminary version of a document, he or she is concentrating on conveying ideas. This preliminary version is called a rough draft. After the draft is created, the writer edits or refines the copy. Proofreaders' marks are used to edit the rough draft. The editing changes will be made to the original. Then the writer reads the copy again. Editing requires a lot of time and effort. An attitude of excellence is required to produce an error-free message.

Lesson 18 | 3 and 6

KEYBOARDING PRO DELUXE 2

WARMUP

Warmup 18a

Key each line twice.

alphabet 1 Jim Kable won a second prize for his very quixotic drawings.
figures 2 If 57 of the 105 boys go on July 29, 48 of them will remain.
easy 3 With the usual bid, I paid for a quantity of big world maps.
| 1 | 2 | 3 | 4 | 5 | 6 | 7 | 8 | 9 | 10 | 11 | 12 |

New Keys

18b 3 and 6

Key each line once.

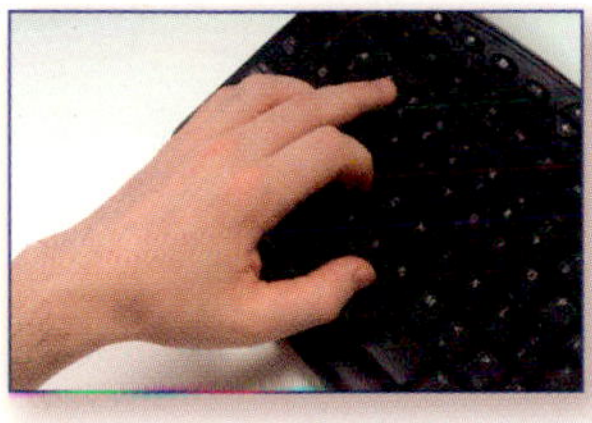

© CENGAGE LEARNING

3 Reach *up* with *left second* finger.

© CENGAGE LEARNING

6 Reach *up* with *right first* finger.

Note: Ergonomic keyboard users will use *left first* finger to key 6.

3

4 3 3d d3 3 3; had 3 days; did 3 dives; led 3 dogs; add 3 dips
5 we 3 ride 3 cars; take 33 dials; read 3 copies; save 33 days
6 On July 3, 33 lights lit 33 stands holding 33 prize winners.

6

7 6 6j 6j 6 6; 6 jays; 6 jams; 6 jigs; 6 jibs; 6 jots; 6 jokes
8 only 6 high; on 66 units; reach 66 numbers; 6 yams or 6 jams
9 On May 6, Car 66 delivered 66 tons of No. 6 shale to Pier 6.

all figures learned

10 At 6 p.m., Channel 3 reported the August 6 score was 6 to 3.
11 Jean, do Items 28 and 6; Mika, 59 and 10; Kyle, 3, 4, and 7.
12 Cars 56 and 34 used Aisle 9; Cars 2 and 87 can use Aisle 10.

Skill Building

18c Keyboard Reinforcement

Key each line once.

TECHNIQUE TIP

Make long reaches without returning to home row between reaches.

long reaches

13 ce cede cedar wreck nu nu nut punt nuisance my my amy mystic
14 ny ny any many company mu mu mull lumber mulch br br furbish
15 Cecil received a large brown umbrella from Bunny and Hunter.

number review

16 set 0; push 4; Car 00; score 44; jot 04; age 40; Billet 4004
17 April 5; lock 5; set 66; fill 55; hit 65; pick 56; adds 5665
18 Her grades are 93, 87, and 100; his included 82, 96, and 54.

Skill Building

25d Textbook Keying

Key each line once; DS between groups.

Key with precision and without hesitation.

13 is if he do rub ant go and am pan do rut us aid ox ape by is
14 it is | an end | it may | to pay | and so | aid us | he got | or own | to go
15 Did the girl make the ornament with fur, duck down, or hair?

16 us owl rug box bob to man so bit or big pen of jay me age it
17 it | it is | time to go | show them how | plan to go | one of the aims
18 It is a shame they use the autobus for a visit to the field.

| 1 | 2 | 3 | 4 | 5 | 6 | 7 | 8 | 9 | 10 | 11 | 12 |

25e Figure Check

In the Word Processor, key two 3' writings at a controlled rate. Save the timings as *xx-25e-t1* and *xx-25e-t2*. **Use wordwrap.**

Goal: 3', 16–14 *gwam*.

E ALL LETTERS/FIGURES

	gwam 3'	
Do I read the stock market pages in the news? Yes; and	4	35
at about 9 or 10 a.m. each morning, I know lots of excited	8	39
people are quick to join me. In fact, many of us zip right	12	43
to the 3rd or 4th part of the paper to see if the prices of	16	47
our stocks have gone up or down. Now, those of us who are	19	51
"speculators" like to "buy at 52 and sell at 60"; while the	23	55
"investors" among us are more interested in a dividend we	27	59
may get, say 7 or 8 percent, than in the price of a stock.	31	62

3' | 1 | 2 | 3 | 4 |

Communication

25f Edited Copy

1. In the Word Processor, key your name, class, and date at the left margin, each on a separate line.
2. Key the paragraphs and make the corrections marked with proofreaders' marks. Use the BACKSPACE key to correct errors.
3. Check all number expressions and correct any mistakes.
4. Save as *xx-25f*.

Last week the healthy heart foundation relased the findings of a study ~~that~~ showed exercise diet and ~~if individuals don'~~t smoke are the major controllable factors that led to a healthy heart. Factors such as heredity can not be controlled. The study included 25 to 65 ~~year old~~ males ~~as well as~~ females.

The study also showed that just taking a walk ~~benefits our health~~. Those who walked an average of 2 to 3 hours a week were more then 30 percent less likely to have problems than those who did no exercise.

18d Textbook Keying

Key each line once; DS between 2-line groups.

word response: *think* and *key* words

19 he el id is go us it an me of he of to if ah or bye do so am

20 Did she enamel emblems on a big panel for the downtown sign?

stroke response: *think* and *key* each stroke

21 kin are hip read lymph was pop saw ink art oil gas up as mop

22 Barbara started the union wage earners tax in Texas in July.

combination response: vary speed but maintain rhythm

23 upon than eve lion when burley with they only them loin were

24 It was the opinion of my neighbor that we may work as usual.

18e Timed Writing

1. Key two 3' writings. **Use wordwrap.**
2. End the lesson but do not exit the software.

Goals: 1', 17–23 *gwam*
2', 15–21 *gwam*
3', 14–20 *gwam*

E ALL LETTERS

	gwam 2'	3'
I am something quite precious. Though millions of people	6	4
in other countries might not have me, you likely do. I have	12	8
a lot of power. For it is I who names a new president every	18	12
four years. It is I who decides if a tax shall be levied.	24	16
I even decide questions of war or peace. I was acquired at	30	20
a great cost; however, I am free to all citizens. And yet,	36	24
sadly, I am often ignored; or, still worse, I am just taken	42	28
for granted. I can be lost, and in certain circumstances I	48	32
can even be taken away. What, you may ask, am I? I am your	54	36
right to vote. Don't take me lightly.	58	39

2' | 1 | 2 | 3 | 4 | 5 | 6 |
3' | 1 | 2 | 3 | 4 |

Communication

18f Composition

1. Go to the Word Processor.
2. Introduce yourself to your instructor by composing two paragraphs, each containing about three sentences. Use proper grammatical structure. Do not worry about keying errors at this time.
3. Save the document as *xx-profile*. (Remember to replace *xx* with your initials.) It is not necessary to print the document. You will open and print it in a later lesson.

Lesson 25 | Assessment

WARMUP

KEYBOARDING PRO DELUXE 2 — Lessons/25a Warmup

Key each line twice.

alphabet 1 My wife helped fix a frozen lock on Jacque's vegetable bins.

figures 2 Sherm moved from 823 West 150th Street to 9472--67th Street.

double letters 3 Will Scotty attempt to sell his accounting books to Elliott?

easy 4 It is a shame he used the endowment for a visit to the city.

| 1 | 2 | 3 | 4 | 5 | 6 | 7 | 8 | 9 | 10 | 11 | 12 |

25b Reach Review

Key each line once; repeat.

TECHNIQUE TIP

Keep arms and hands quiet as you practice the long reaches.

n/y

5 deny many canny tiny nymph puny any puny zany penny pony yen

6 Jenny Nyles saw many, many tiny nymphs flying near her pony.

b/r

7 bran barb brim curb brat garb bray verb brag garb bribe herb

8 Barb Barber can bring a bit of bran and herbs for her bread.

c/e

9 cede neck nice deck dice heck rice peck vice erect mice echo

10 Can Cecil erect a decent cedar deck? He erects nice condos.

n/u

11 nun gnu bun nut pun numb sun nude tuna nub fun null unit gun

12 Eunice had enough ground nuts at lunch; Uncle Launce is fun.

25c Timed Writing

Key two 3' writings. Strive for accuracy. **Use wordwrap.**

Goal: 3', 19–27 *gwam.*

E ALL LETTERS

gwam 3'

The term careers can mean many different things to 3 | 51
different people. As you know, a career is much more than a 8 | 55
job. It is the kind of work that a person has through life. 12 | 59
It includes the jobs a person has over time. It also involves 16 | 63
how the work life affects the other parts of our life. There 20 | 67
are as many types of careers as there are people. 23 | 71

Almost all people have a career of some kind. A career 27 | 74
can help us to reach unique goals, such as to make a living 31 | 79
or to help others. The kind of career you have will affect 35 | 83
your life in many ways. For example, it can determine where 39 | 87
you live, the money you make, and how you feel about yourself. 44 | 91
A good choice can thus help you realize the life you want. 47 | 95

3' | 1 | 2 | 3 | 4 |

Lesson 19 | $ and - (hyphen), Number Expression

KEYBOARDING PRO DELUXE 2

WARMUP

Warmup 19a

Key each line twice.

alphabet 1 Why did the judge quiz poor Victor about his blank tax form?

figures 2 J. Boyd, Ph.D., changed Items 10, 57, 36, and 48 on page 92.

3rd row 3 To try the tea, we hope to tour the port prior to the party.

easy 4 Did he signal the authentic robot to do a turn to the right?

| 1 | 2 | 3 | 4 | 5 | 6 | 7 | 8 | 9 | 10 | 11 | 12 |

New Keys

19b $ and -

Key each line once; DS between 2-line groups.

- = hyphen
-- = dash
Do not space before or after a hyphen or a dash.

$ Shift; then reach *up* with *left first* finger.

- (hyphen) Reach *up* with *right fourth* finger.

$

5 $ $f f$ $ $; if $4; half $4; off $4; of $4; $4 fur; $4 flats

6 for $8; cost $9; log $3; grab $10; give Rolf $2; give Viv $4

7 Since she paid $45 for the item priced at $54, she saved $9.

- (hyphen)

8 - -; ;- - - -; up-to-date; co-op; father-in-law; four-square

9 pop-up foul; big-time job; snap-on bit; one- or two-hour ski

10 You need 6 signatures--half of the members--on the petition.

all symbols learned

11 I paid $10 for the low-cost disk; high-priced ones cost $40.

12 Le-An spent $20 for travel, $95 for books, and $38 for food.

13 Mr. Loft-Smit sold his boat for $467; he bought it for $176.

Skill Building

19c Keyboard Reinforcement

Key each line once; repeat the drill.

e/d 14 Edie discreetly decided to deduct expenses in making a deal.

w/e 15 Working women wear warm wool sweaters when weather dictates.

r/e 16 We heard very rude remarks regarding her recent termination.

s/d 17 Daily sudden mishaps destroyed several dozens of sand dunes.

v/b 18 Beverley voted by giving a bold beverage to every brave boy.

Skill Building

24c Rhythm Builder

Key each line once.

double letters
17 feel pass mill good miss seem moons cliffs pools green spell
18 Assets are being offered in a stuffy room to two associates.

balanced hand
19 is if of to it go do to is do so if to to the it sign vie to
20 Pamela Fox may wish to go to town with Blanche if she works.

one hand
21 date face ere bat lip sew lion rear brag fact join eggs ever
22 get fewer on; after we look; as we agree; add debt; act fast

combination
23 was for | in the case of | they were | to down | mend it | but pony is
24 They were to be down in the fastest sleigh if you are right.

| 1 | 2 | 3 | 4 | 5 | 6 | 7 | 8 | 9 | 10 | 11 | 12 |

24d Timed Writing

Take a 3' timing on both paragraphs. **Use wordwrap.** Repeat.

	gwam 1'	3'	
Why don't we like change very much? Do you think that	11	4	26
just maybe we want to be lazy; to dodge new things; and, as	23	8	30
much as possible, not to make hard decisions?	32	11	33
We know change can and does extend new areas for us to	11	14	36
enjoy, areas we might never have known existed; and to stay	24	18	40
away from all change could curtail our quality of life.	34	22	44

1' | 1 | 2 | 3 | 4 | 5 | 6 | 7 | 8 | 9 | 10 | 11 | 12 |
3' | 1 | 2 | 3 | 4 |

24e Edited Copy

1. In the Word Processor, key your name, class, and date at the left margin, each on a separate line.
2. Key each line, making the corrections marked with proofreaders' marks.
3. Correct errors using the BACKSPACE key.
4. Save as *xx-24e*.

```
25 Ask Group 1 to read Chater 6 of Book 11 (Shelf 19,Room 5).
26 All 6 of us live at One Bay road, not at 126-56th Street.
27 AT 9 a.m. the owners decided to close form 12 noon to 1 p.m.
28 Ms. Vik leaves June 9; she r eturns the 14 or 15 of July.
29 The 16 per cent discount saves 115.  A stamp costs 44 cents.
30 Elin gave $300,000,000; our gift was only 75 cents.
```

Communication

24f Composition

1. In the Word Processor, open the file *xx-profile* that you created in Lesson 18.
2. Position the insertion point at the end of the last paragraph. TAP ENTER twice.
3. Key an additional paragraph that begins with the following sentence:

   Thank you for allowing me to introduce myself.
4. Finish the paragraph by adding two or more sentences that describe your progress and satisfaction with keyboarding.
5. Correct any mistakes you have made. Click Save to resave the document. Print.
6. Mark any mistakes you missed with proofreaders' marks. Revise the document, save, and reprint. Submit to your instructor.

19d Textbook Keying

Key each line once, working for fluid, consistent stroking.

TECHNIQUE TIP

- Key the easy words as "words" rather than stroke by stroke.
- Key each phrase (marked by a vertical line) without pauses between words.

easy words

19 am it go bus dye jam irk six sod tic yam ugh spa vow aid dug

20 he or by air big elf dog end fit and lay sue toe wit own got

21 six foe pen firm also body auto form down city kept make fog

easy phrases

22 it is | if the | and also | to me | the end | to us | if it | it is | to the

23 if it is | to the end | do you wish | to go to | for the end | to make

24 lay down | he or she | make me | by air | end of | by me | kept it | of me

easy sentences

25 Did the chap work to mend the torn right half of the ensign?

26 Blame me for their penchant for the antique chair and panel.

27 She bid by proxy for eighty bushels of a corn and rye blend.

Communication

19e Textbook Keying

1. Study the rules and examples at the right.
2. Key the sample sentences 28–33.
3. Change figures to words as needed in sentences 34–36.

NUMBER EXPRESSION: SPELL OUT NUMBERS

1. **First word in a sentence.** Key numbers ten and lower as words unless they are part of a series of related numbers, any of which are over ten.

   Three of the four members were present.

   She wrote 12 stories and 2 plays in five years.

2. The **smaller of two adjacent numbers** as words.

   SolVir shipped six 24-ton engines.

3. **Isolated fractions and approximate numbers.** Key as words **large round numbers that can be expressed as one or two words**. Hyphenate fractions expressed as words.

   She completed one-fourth of the experiments.

   Val sent out three hundred invitations.

4. **Preceding "o'clock."**

   John's due at four o'clock. Pick him up at 4:15 p.m.

28 **Six** or **seven** older players were cut from the **37**-member team.

29 I have **2** of **14** coins I need to start my set. Kristen has **9**.

30 Of **nine 24**-ton engines ordered, we shipped **six** last Tuesday.

31 Shelly has read just **one-half** of about **forty-five** documents.

32 The **six** boys sent well over **two hundred** printed invitations.

33 **One** or **two** of us will be on duty from **two** until **six** o'clock.

34 The meeting begins promptly at 9. We plan 4 sessions.

35 The three-person crew cleaned 6 stands, 12 tables, and 13 desks.

36 The 3rd meeting is at 3 o'clock on Friday, February 2.

Lesson 24 | Other Symbols

WARMUP

KEYBOARDING PRO DELUXE 2 — *Lessons/24a Warmup*

Key each line twice.

alphabet 1 Pfc. Jim Kings covered each of the lazy boxers with a quilt.

figures 2 Do problems 6 to 29 on page 175 before class at 8:30, May 4.

" 3 They read the poems "September Rain" and "The Lower Branch."

easy 4 When did the busy girls fix the tight cowl of the ruby gown?

| 1 | 2 | 3 | 4 | 5 | 6 | 7 | 8 | 9 | 10 | 11 | 12 |

New Keys

24b Textbook Keying

@ < > * + = [ ]

Key each pair of lines once; DS between 2-line groups.

Become familiar with these symbols:

- @ at
- < less than
- > greater than
- * asterisk
- + plus sign (use a hyphen for minus and x for "times")
- = equals
- [ ] left and right bracket

@ shift; reach *up* with *left third* finger to @

5 @ @s s@ @ @; 24 @ .15; 22 @ .35; sold 2 @ .87; were 12 @ .95

6 You may contact Luke @: LJP@rx.com or fax @ (602) 555-0101.

< shift; reach *down* with *right second* finger to <
> shift; reach *down* with *right third* finger to >

7 Can you prove "a > b"? If 28 > 5, then 5a < x. Is a < > b?

8 E-mail Al ajj@crewl.com and Matt mrw10@scxs.com by 9:30 p.m.

* shift; reach *up* with *right second* finger to *

9 * *k k8* * *; aurelis*; May 7*; both sides*; 250 km.**; aka*

10 Note each *; one * refers to page 29; ** refers to page 307.

+ shift; reach *up* with *right fourth* finger to +

11 + ;+ +; + + +; 2 + 2; A+ or B+; 70+ F. degrees; +xy over +y;

12 The question was 8 + 7 + 51; it should have been 8 + 7 + 15.

= reach *up* with *right fourth* finger to =

13 = =; = = =; = 4; If 14x = 28, x = 2; if 8x = 16, then x = 2.

14 Change this solution (where it says "= by") to = bx or = BX.

[ ] reach *up* with *right fourth* finger to [and]

15 Mr. Wing was named. [That's John J. Wing, ex-senator. Ed.]

16 We [Joseph and I] will be in Suite #349; call us @ 555-0102.

Lesson 20 | # and /

KEYBOARDING PRO DELUXE 2

WARMUP

Warmup 20a

Key each line twice (slowly, then faster).

alphabet 1 Freda Jencks will have money to buy six quite large topazes.
symbols 2 I bought 10 ribbons and 45 disks from Cable-Han Co. for $78.
home row 3 Dallas sold jade flasks; Sal has a glass flask full of salt.
easy 4 He may cycle down to the field by the giant oak and cut hay.

New Keys

20b # and /

Key each line once.

= number sign, pounds
/ = diagonal, slash

© CENGAGE LEARNING

Shift; then reach *up* with *left second* finger.

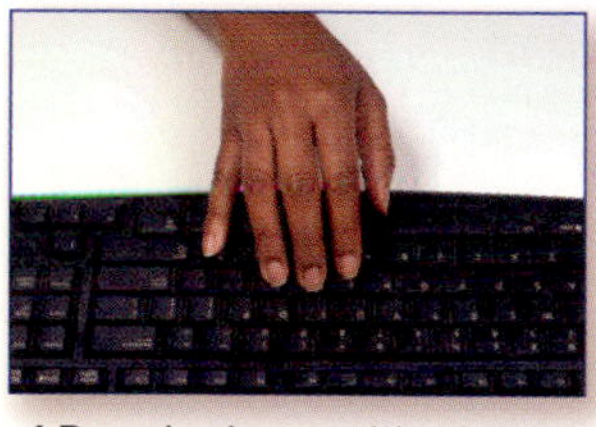

© CENGAGE LEARNING

/ Reach *down* with *right fourth* finger.

#

5 # #e e# # # #; had #3 dial; did #3 drop; set #3 down; Bid #3
6 leave #82; sold #20; Lyric #16; bale #34; load #53; Optic #7
7 Notice #333 says to load Car #33 with 33# of #3 grade shale.

/

8 / /; ;/ / / /; 1/2; 1/3; Mr./Mrs.; 1/4/12; 22 11/12; and/or;
9 to/from; /s/ William Smit; 2/10, n/30; his/her towels; 6 1/2
10 The numerals 1 5/8, 3 1/4, and 60 7/9 are “mixed fractions.”

all symbols learned

11 Invoice #737 cites 15 2/3# of rye was shipped C.O.D. 4/6/11.
12 B-O-A Company’s Check #50/5 for $87 paid for 15# of #3 wire.
13 Our Co-op List #20 states $40 for 16 1/2 crates of tomatoes.

Skill Building

20c Keyboard Reinforcement

Key each line once; work for fluency.

Option: In the Word Processor, key 30" writings on both lines of a pair. Work to avoid pauses.

	gwam 30"
14 She did the key work at the height of the problem.	20
15 Form #726 is the title to the island; she owns it.	20
16 The rock is a form of fuel; he did enrich it with coal.	22
17 The corn-and-turkey dish is a blend of turkey and corn.	22
18 It is right to work to end the social problems of the world.	24
19 If I sign it on 3/19, the form can aid us to pay the 40 men.	24

Skill Building

23d Textbook Keying

Key each line once; work for fluency.

20 *Jane may work with an auditing firm if she is paid to do so.*
21 *Pam and eight girls may go to the lake to work with the dog.*
22 *Clancy and Claudia did all the work to fix the sign problem.*
23 *Did Lea visit the Orlando land of enchantment or a neighbor?*
24 *Ana and Blanche made a map for a neighbor to go to the city.*
25 *Sidney may go to the lake to fish with worms from the docks.*
26 *Did the firm or the neighbors own the auto with the problem?*

| 1 | 2 | 3 | 4 | 5 | 6 | 7 | 8 | 9 | 10 | 11 | 12 |

23e Timed Writing

Take a 3' timing on both paragraphs. **Use wordwrap.** Repeat.

E ALL LETTERS

	gwam 1'	3'	
Is how you judge my work important? It is, of course;	11	4	26
I hope you recognize some basic merit in it. We all expect	23	8	30
to get credit for good work that we conclude.	32	11	33
I want approval for stands I take, things I write, and	11	14	36
work I complete. My efforts, by my work, show a picture of	23	18	41
me; thus, through my work, I am my own unique creation.	34	22	44

1' | 1 | 2 | 3 | 4 | 5 | 6 | 7 | 8 | 9 | 10 | 11 | 12 |
3' | 1 | 2 | 3 | 4 |

Communication

23f Edit Text

1. Read the information about proofreaders' marks.
2. In the Word Processor, key your name, class, and **23f** at the left margin. Then key lines 27–32, making the revisions as you key. Use the BACKSPACE key to correct errors.
3. Save as *xx-23f* and print.

Proofreaders' marks are used to identify mistakes in typed or printed text. Learn to apply these commonly used standard proofreaders' marks.

Symbol	Meaning	Symbol	Meaning
____	Italic	○ sp	Spell out
~~	Bold	¶	Paragraph
Cap or ≡	Capitalize	#	Add horizontal space
^	Insert	/ or lc	Lowercase
↗	Delete	⁀	Close up space
⊏	Move to left	∼	Transpose
⊐	Move to right	stet	Leave as originally written

27 We miss 50% in life's rowards by refusingto new try things.

28 do it now--today--then tomorrow's load will be 100%% lighter.

29 Satisfying work-whether it pays $40 or $400-is the pay off.

30 Avoid mistakes: confusing a #3 has cost thousands.

31 Pleased most with a first-rate job is the person who did it.

32 My wife and/or me mother will except the certifi cate for me.

Communication

20d Textbook Keying: Number Usage Review

Key each line once. Decide whether the circled numbers should be keyed as figures or as words and make needed changes. Check your finished work with 19e, page 47.

```
20 Six or (7) older players were cut from the (37)-member team.
21 I have (2) of 14 coins I need to start my set.  Kristen has (9).
22 Of (9) 24-ton engines ordered, we shipped (6) last Tuesday.
23 Shelly has read just (1) half of about (45) documents.
24 The (6) boys sent well over (200) printed invitations.
25 (1) or (2) of us will be on duty from (2) until (6) o'clock.
```

Skill Building

E ALL LETTERS

20e Timed Writing

1. Take a 3' writing on both paragraphs. If you finish the timing before time is up, repeat the timing. **Use wordwrap.**
2. End the lesson but do not exit the software.

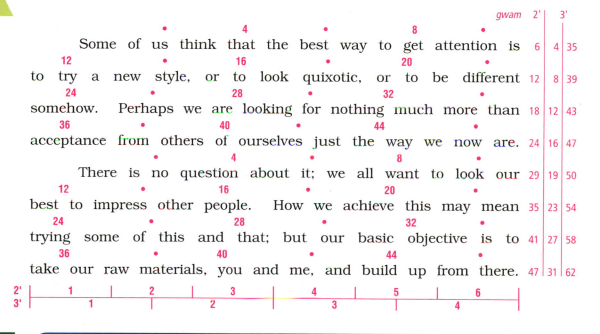

	gwam	2'	3'
Some of us think that the best way to get attention is	6	4	35
to try a new style, or to look quixotic, or to be different	12	8	39
somehow. Perhaps we are looking for nothing much more than	18	12	43
acceptance from others of ourselves just the way we now are.	24	16	47
There is no question about it; we all want to look our	29	19	50
best to impress other people. How we achieve this may mean	35	23	54
trying some of this and that; but our basic objective is to	41	27	58
take our raw materials, you and me, and build up from there.	47	31	62

20f Guided Writing

Go to the Word Processor, and follow the directions at the right to build your speed on each paragraph of the timing by four words.

Goal: 16 *gwam*

1/4'	1/2'	3/4'	*gwam* 1'
4	8	12	16
5	10	15	20
6	12	18	24
7	14	21	28
8	16	24	32
9	18	27	36
10	20	30	40

STANDARD PLAN for Guided Writing Procedures

1. In the Word Processor, take a 1' writing on paragraph 1. Note your *gwam*.
2. Add four words to your 1' *gwam* to determine your goal rate.
3. Set the Timer for 1'. Set the Timer option to beep every 15".
4. From the table below, select from column 4 the speed nearest your goal rate. Note the ¼' point at the left of that speed. Place a light check mark within the paragraphs at the ¼' points.
5. Take two 1' guided writings on paragraphs 1 and 2. Do not save.
6. Turn the beeper off.

Lesson 23 | & and : (colon), Proofreaders' Marks

WARMUP

KEYBOARDING PRO DELUXE 2 — *Lessons/23a Warmup*

Key each line twice.

alphabet 1 Roxy waved as she did quick flying jumps on the trapeze bar.
symbols 2 Ryan's--with an A-1 rating--sold Item #146 (for $10) on 2/7.
space bar 3 Mr. Fyn may go to Cape Cod on the bus, or he may go by auto.
easy 4 Susie is busy; may she halt the social work for the auditor?
| 1 | 2 | 3 | 4 | 5 | 6 | 7 | 8 | 9 | 10 | 11 | 12 |

New Keys

23b & and : (colon)

Key each line once.

& = ampersand: The ampersand is used only as part of company names.

Colon: Space twice after a colon except when used within a number for time.

© CENGAGE LEARNING

& Shift; then reach *up* with *right first* finger.

© CENGAGE LEARNING

: (colon) Left shift; then tap key with *right fourth* finger.

& (ampersand)

5 & &j j& & & &; J & J; Haraj & Jay; Moroj & Jax; Torj & Jones
6 Nehru & Unger; Mumm & Just; Mann & Hart; Arch & Jones; M & J
7 Rhye & Knox represent us; Steb & Doy, Firm A; R & J, Firm B.

: (colon)

8 : :; :; : : :; as: for example: notice: To: From: Date:
9 in stock: 8:30; 7:45; Age: Experience: Read: Send: See:
10 Space twice after a colon, thus: To: No.: Time: Carload:

all symbols learned

11 Consider these companies: J & R, Brand & Kay, Uper & Davis.
12 Memo #88-89 reads as follows: "Deduct 15% of $300, or $45."
13 Bill 32(5)--it got here quite late--from M & N was paid 7/3.

23c Keyboard Reinforcement

Key each line twice; work for fluency.

double letters

14 Di Bennett was puzzled by drivers exceeding the speed limit.
15 Bill needs the office address; he will cut the grass at ten.
16 Todd saw the green car veer off the street near a tall tree.

figures and symbols

17 Invoice #84 for $672.90, plus $4.38 tax, was due on 5/19/11.
18 Do read Section 4, pages 60-74 and Section 9, pages 198-225.
19 Enter the following: (a) name, (b) address, and (c) tax ID.

Lesson 21 | % and !

WARMUP

KEYBOARDING PRO DELUXE 2 — *Lessons/21a Warmup*

Key each line twice.

alphabet 1 Merry will have picked out a dozen quarts of jam for boxing.
fig/sym 2 Jane-Ann bought 16 7/8 yards of #240 cotton at $3.59 a yard.
1st row 3 Can't brave, zany Cave Club men/women next climb Mt. Zamban?
easy 4 Did she rush to cut six bushels of corn for the civic corps?

New Keys

21b % and !

Key each line once.

% = percent sign: Use % with business forms or where space is restricted; otherwise, use the word "percent."

Space twice after the exclamation point!

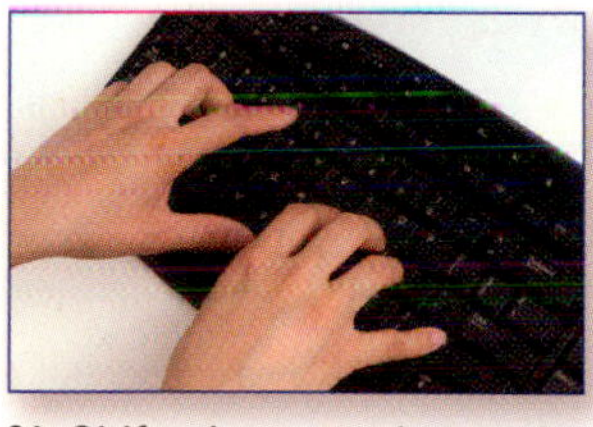

% Shift; then reach *up* with *left first* finger.

%

5 % %f f% % %; off 5%; if 5%; of 5% fund; half 5%; taxes of 5%
6 7% rent; 3% tariff; 9% F.O.B.; 15% greater; 28% base; up 46%
7 Give discounts of 5% on rods, 50% on lures, and 75% on line.

! reach *up* with the *left fourth* finger

8 ! !a a! ! ! !; Eureka! Ha! No! Pull 10! Extra! America!
9 Listen to the call! Now! Ready! Get set! Go! Good show!
10 I want it now, not next week! I am sure to lose 50% or $19.

all symbols

11 The ad offers a 10% discount, but this notice says 15% less!
12 He got the job! With Clark's Supermarket! Please call Mom!
13 Bill #92-44 arrived very late from Zyclone; it was paid 7/4.

SPACING TIP

- Do not space between a figure and the % or $ signs.
- Do not space before or after the dash.

21c Keyboard Reinforcement

Key each line once; work for fluency.

all symbols

14 As of 6/28, Jeri owes $31 for dinner and $27 for cab fare.
15 Invoice #20--it was dated 3/4--billed $17 less 15% discount.
16 He deducted 2% instead of 6%, a clear saving of 6% vs. 7%.

combination response

17 Look at my dismal grade in English; but I guess I earned it.
18 Kris started to blend a cocoa beverage for a shaken cowhand.
19 Jan may make a big profit if she owns the title to the land.

22d Timed Writing

1. Take a 3' timing on both paragraphs.
2. End the lesson; then go to the Word Processor and complete 22e and 22f.

	1'	3'	
Most people will agree that we owe it to our children	10	4	28
to pass the planet on to them in better condition than we	22	7	32
found it. We must take extra steps just to make the quality	34	12	36
of living better.	38	13	37
If we do not change our ways quickly and stop damaging	11	16	41
our world, it will not be a good place to live. We can save	12	21	45
the ozone and wildlife and stop polluting the air and water.	35	25	49

1' | 1 | 2 | 3 | 4 | 5 | 6 | 7 | 8 | 9 | 10 | 11 | 12 |
3' | 1 | 2 | 3 | 4 |

Skill Building

22e BACKSPACE Key

In the Word Processor, key the sentences using the BACKSPACE key to correct errors.

18 You should be interested in the special items on sale today.
19 If she is going with us, why don't we plan to leave now?
20 Do you desire to continue working on the memo in the future?
21 Did the firm or their neighbors own the autos with problems?
22 Juni, Vec, and Zeb had perfect grades on weekly query exams.
23 Jewel quickly explained to me the big fire hazards involved.

Communication

22f Word Processor

1. Study the rules and examples at the right.
2. In the Word Processor, key the information below at the left margin. Tap ENTER as shown.
   Your name ENTER
   Current date ENTER
   Number Expression ENTER
3. Key the sample sentences 24–28. If you make an error, backspace to correct it.
4. Save the file as *xx-22f*.

NUMBER EXPRESSION: EXPRESS AS FIGURES

1. **Money amounts and percentages, even when appoximate.** Spell out cents and percent except in statistical copy.

   The 16 percent discount saved me $145; Bill, 95 cents.

2. **Round numbers expressed in millions or higher with their word modifier.**

   Ms. Ti contributed $3 million.

3. **House numbers** (except house number One) and street names over ten. If a street name is a number, separate it from the house number with a dash.

   1510 Easy Street   One West Ninth Avenue   1592--11th Street

4. **Date following a month.** A date preceding the month is expressed in figures followed by "rd" or "th."

   June 9, 2009   March 3   4th of July

5. **Numbers used with nouns.**

   Volume 1   Chapter 6

24 Ask **Group 2** to read **Chapter 7** of **Book 11** (**Shelf 19, Room 5**).
25 All **six** of us live at **One Bay Lane**, not at **142--59th Street**.
26 At **8 a.m.** the owners decided to close from **12 noon** to **1 p.m.**
27 Ms. Han leaves **June 3**; she returns the **14th or 15th of July**.
28 The **16 percent** discount saves **$115**. A stamp costs **44 cents**.

Skill Building

21d Textbook Keying

Key each line once; DS between groups; fingers curved, hands quiet. Repeat if time permits.

1st finger

20 by bar get fun van for inn art from gray hymn July true verb
21 brag human bring unfold hominy mighty report verify puny joy
22 You are brave to try bringing home the van in the bad storm.

2nd finger

23 ace ink did cad keyed deep seed kind Dick died kink like kid
24 cease decease decades kick secret check decide kidney evaded
25 Dedre likes the idea of ending dinner with cake for dessert.

3rd finger

26 oil sow six vex wax axe low old lox pool west loss wool slow
27 swallow swamp saw sew wood sax sexes loom stew excess school
28 Wes waxes floors and washes windows at low costs to schools.

4th finger

29 zap zip craze pop pup pan daze quote queen quiz pizza puzzle
30 zoo graze zipper panzer zebra quip partizan patronize appear
31 Czar Zane appears to be dazzled by the apple pizza and jazz.

21e Timed Writing

1. Key a 2' writing. Repeat.
2. End the lesson but do not exit the software.
3. Go to the Word Processor and complete 21f.

Goal: 16 *gwam*

E ALL LETTERS

	gwam 1'	2'	
Teams are the basic unit of performance for a firm.	11	5	42
They are not the solution to all of the organizational needs.	23	12	48
They will not solve all of the problems, but it is known	35	17	54
that a team can perform at a higher rate than other groups.	47	23	60
It is one of the best ways to support the changes needed for	59	30	66
a firm. The team must have time in order to make	71	36	72
a quality working plan.	74	37	74

1' | 1 | 2 | 3 | 4 | 5 | 6 | 7 | 8 | 9 | 10 | 11 | 12 |
2' | 1 | 2 | 3 | 4 | 5 | 6 |

21f Speed Runs with Numbers

1. Set the Timer in the Word Processor for 1'.
2. Take two 1' writings; the last number you key when you stop is your approximate *gwam*. Do not save.

1 and 2 and 3 and 4 and 5 and 6 and 7 and 8 and 9 and 10 and 11 and 12 and 13 and 14 and 15 and 16 and 17 and 18 and 19 and 20 and 21 and 22 and 23 and 24 and 25 and 26 and 27 and

Lesson 22 | (and) and Backspace Key

WARMUP

KEYBOARDING PRO DELUXE 2 — *Lessons/22a Warmup*

Key each line twice.

alphabet 1 Avoid lazy punches; expert fighters jab with a quick motion.
fig/sym 2 Be-Low's Bill #483/7 was $96.90, not $102--they took 5% off.
caps lock 3 Report titles may be shown in ALL CAPS; as, BOLD WORD POWER.
easy 4 Do they blame me for their dismal social and civic problems?

| 1 | 2 | 3 | 4 | 5 | 6 | 7 | 8 | 9 | 10 | 11 | 12 |

New Keys

22b (and) (parentheses)

Key each line once.

( ) = parentheses
Parentheses indicate off-hand, aside, or explanatory messages.

© CENGAGE LEARNING

(Shift; then reach *up* with the *right third* finger.

© CENGAGE LEARNING

) Shift; then reach *up* with the *right fourth* finger.

5 ((l l((; (; Reach from l for the left parenthesis; as, ((.
6)); ;))); Reach from ; for the right parenthesis; as,)).

( )

7 Learn to use parentheses (plural) or parenthesis (singular).
8 The red (No. 34) and blue (No. 78) cars both won here (Rio).
9 We (Galen and I) dined (bagels) in our penthouse (the dorm).

all symbols learned

10 The jacket was $35 (thirty-five dollars)--the tie was extra.
11 Starting 10/29, you can sell Model #49 at a discount of 25%.
12 My size 8 1/2 shoe--a blue pump--was soiled (but not badly).

22c Textbook Keying

Key each line once, keeping eyes on copy.

13 Jana has one hard-to-get copy of her hot-off-the-press book.
14 An invoice said that "We give discounts of 10%, 5%, and 3%."
15 The company paid bill 8/07 on 5/2/11 and bill 4/9 on 3/6/11.
16 The catalog lists as out of stock Items #230, #710, and #13.
17 Elyn had $8; Sean, $9; and Cal, $7. The cash total was $24.

Reference Guide

Digital Citizenship

OVERVIEW

One search using a popular search engine and *digital citizenship* as keywords produced over three million results. A quick survey of the list of documents indicated that digital citizenship is a popular, if not required, topic in the curricula of K-12 schools. Many of the documents focused on digital citizenship research by Dr. Mike Ribble, on the framework developed by the Partnership for 21st Century Skills, and on the International Society for Technology in Education Standards for Students. A relatively small percentage of the documents listed referred to collegiate education or business and industry.

This article focuses on effective digital citizenship from four perspectives that can affect your career.

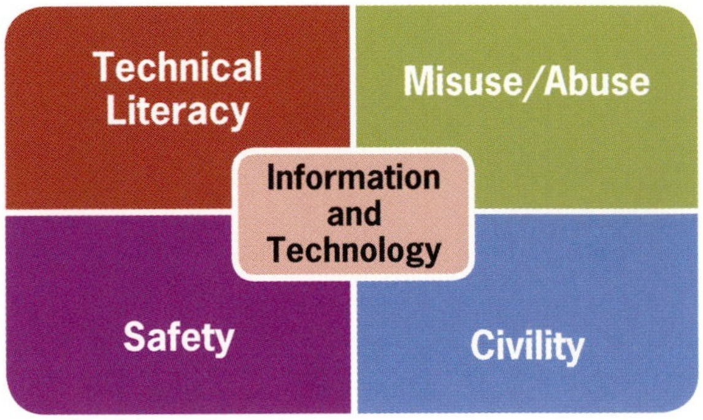

TECHNICAL LITERACY

Understanding how the Internet, Web 2.0 applications, and other digital tools work enables you to use these tools creatively, responsibly, and safely. Technology is constantly evolving; things learned today can be outdated in a very short time. Therefore, continual learning is the only way to keep up with technology. Protecting your (or your company's) computer, network, and information from unauthorized access is critical. Many students and young employees who have grown up using all types of technology may be more technically savvy than their instructors or their managers. However, they often do not have the social skills and business savvy to be effective in using digital tools.

MISUSE/ABUSE

The Internet is a vast collection of information that can be accessed easily and at little or no cost. However, just because information has been posted on the Internet does not mean that it is accurate or valid.

Information Verification. Information should be analyzed carefully to determine the credibility of the writer, source of the information, accuracy of details, knowledge of the literature, and the currency of the information before relying on that information.

Plagiarism. Copyright laws protect material from unauthorized use. Request permission before using copyrighted materials. It is not acceptable to copy information from the Internet without properly documenting the source of the information and giving the writer proper credit. Software is available to check a paper and quickly determine if it has been plagiarized.

Piracy. Downloading of music, games, and movies and making copies of software without permission are illegal.

SAFETY

Privacy. Protecting private information and company proprietary information are key safety concerns. Protect your information and/or your company's information by using up-to-date antivirus software, antispyware, and firewalls.

Identity theft. Unauthorized persons may obtain information such as your Social Security number or credit card information and use it for criminal purposes. Posting private information on social networks can have serious negative consequences as shown in the following examples.

- Posting pictures of vacation sites and travel information alerted criminals that the family was away and their home was robbed.
- Posting pictures of children on the Internet and address information in other locations attracted predators to the home.
- Unprofessional information and pictures on a social network were viewed by a potential employer causing the person not to be hired. Many employers check out potential employees on social networks before hiring them.
- Negative information posted about a person's supervisor and company was viewed by company executives.

CIVILITY

Courtesy and good manners when posting information, sending e-mails, participating in a chat room, blogging, or posting on a social media site are always appropriate. The following tips are examples of good *netiquette*.

© iSTOCKPHOTO/ IZVORINKA JANKOVIC

- Consider anything you post to be public information. Many people use technology to deliver messages that they would never send in a face-to-face situation.
- Use appropriate, non-offensive language and be sensitive to cultural issues.
- Avoid inflammatory messages and messages keyed in all capital letters.
- Be helpful to people who have less technical expertise than you do. They may have great ideas even though they are not technically savvy.
- Avoid texting and checking and sending e-mails, and place cell phones on vibrate during meetings and dining.

Keyboarding—Bridge to Today's Technology

WHO NEEDS A KEYBOARD WITH TODAY'S TECHNOLOGY?

This question is frequently asked and framed in many ways. Often it takes the form of: Are keyboarding skills still valid and necessary with touch, pen, and voice technology available? When asked a similar question relating to small devices, Microsoft co-founder Bill Gates had this to say about it: "I'm a big believer in touch and digital reading, but I still think that some mixture of voice, the pen, and a real keyboard—in other words a netbook—will be the mainstream on that." (www.electronista.com/articles/10/02/10; picture source: Microsoft Board of Directors webpage).

The most frequent answer to the question is that everyone who needs a computer in their lives or in their jobs needs keyboarding skill. It is simply a prerequisite for effective and productive use of today's technology. Note the keywords—effective and productive use. Individuals who do not have effective touch keyboarding skills are at a significant disadvantage using today's technology. It is clear that the self-taught hunt and peck system is neither adequate nor acceptable. Voice technology, pen technology, the mouse, and touch technology have been in existence for a number of years and, for many years, have been predicted to replace keyboarding skill. Yet, market penetration for those skills in business offices is negligible. The need for keyboarding skills continues to flourish, and the investment in developing keyboarding skills continues to be a wise one.

WHAT JOBS REQUIRE COMPUTERS (AND THUS KEYBOARDING SKILLS)?

A number of years ago, keyboarding skills were often thought of as clerical skills. Today, most estimates show that keyboarding skills are communication and technical skills used in more than 90 percent of all jobs. Careers that are enhanced significantly by keyboarding skills include medical, legal, business, journalism, scientific, engineering, teaching, and numerous other fields.

The keyboard is likely to be the primary input device for computers for many years to come. Learn to use it effectively!

Technology and Your Health

YOU ARE IN CHARGE!

Medical self-management is a very popular concept in the prevention, treatment, and control of diseases, such as chronic pain, diabetes, asthma, stress, high blood pressure, and many others. Patients can be trained to prevent, treat, and control many of the symptoms and problems caused by these diseases. If fact, some patients become more effective managing their disease than their medical staff. A number of health issues may be associated with the use of technology, but nobody is in a better position to prevent and manage these issues than you are. The most important concept to remember is that prevention is far more effective than curing health issues.

TECHNOLOGY HEALTH ISSUES

Many computer users are quick to blame the monitor, keyboard, and mouse for eye strain, repetitive stress injuries (RSI), cumulative trauma disorders (CTDs), and carpal tunnel syndrome (CTS). The appropriate question is: Is the technology the cause of the problems or is the real culprit the way the technology is set up and used?

© ISTOCKPHOTO/ JUSTIN HORROCKS

SUSIE VANHUSS

LOU CYPHER/JUPITERIMAGES

Which of the three extensive computer users pictured here is least likely to experience some of the issues listed above?

The user in the center is least likely to experience some of the issues listed above for several reasons:

- He is the only one not using a laptop. Laptops are difficult to position comfortably because the screen and keyboard are both attached. With a laptop, typically the screen is too low or the keyboard is too high.
- With the desktop computer, the screen is large and is positioned at a comfortable height and distance; the keyboard is at the correct height and the mouse is next to it.
- The user's posture, hand, and arm position are correct.
- The user on the left is likely to experience muscular discomfort because the position of the laptop requires him to lean forward and extend his arms.
- The user on the right is likely to experience eye fatigue because of glare from the window he is facing and because the screen is too low; his posture may also cause some muscular fatigue.

SET UP YOUR WORK ENVIRONMENT

The setup depends on the physical size of the individual and the type of computer being used.

Laptops

Laptop computers are not designed ergonomically. They are fine for occasional use, but are not as effective for extensive computer use. Laptops used extensively are best set up with a docking station which allows the user to plug in a separate monitor and/or a separate keyboard. The laptop can then be set up in the same manner that a desktop computer is set up.

Desktop Computers

The position of the monitor, keyboard, mouse, and chair are important. A few guides to follow:

- Position the screen so that the top is at about eye level and about arm's length from the user. Avoid glare from windows if possible. Increase the size of the text and icons on the screen if necessary.
- The keyboard tray should be positioned so that it is about two inches above your thighs and your arms are parallel to the floor.
- The mouse should be positioned close to the keyboard.
- Adjust the chair to a comfortable position.

POSITION THE USER APPROPRIATELY

Correct posture and hand position are important. Moving around and frequent breaks are also important. Exercises to relax your eyes and strengthen your fingers and muscles are also helpful. The videos in your *Keyboarding Pro* software demonstrate good posture and setting up the environment.

- Sit upright in the chair and face the computer; feet should be flat on the floor.
- Arms should be parallel to the floor and wrists straight.
- Position the arms close to the body.
- User position should be such that extended reaching is not necessary.

RESOURCES

Excellent information on ergonomics for computer workstations is available from the Department of Occupational Health and Safety. The website also provides a series of stretches and exercises. Visit the website at:

http://dohs.ors.od.nih.gov/ergo_computers.htm.

Windows 7 and File Management

Section 1 | *Microsoft Windows 7*

OVERVIEW

Windows 7 is the newest operating system software released by Microsoft. The operating system software controls the operations of the computer and works with the application software. *Windows 7* works with *Word* in opening, printing, deleting, and saving files. It also allows you to work with photos and pictures, play music, and access the Internet.

When you turn on your computer, *Windows* displays a login screen followed by a password screen. See your instructor for login and password information. The *Windows 7* desktop displays after you have logged in.

MICROSOFT WINDOWS 7 DESKTOP

TIP

The Windows desktop and its components are described on the next page.

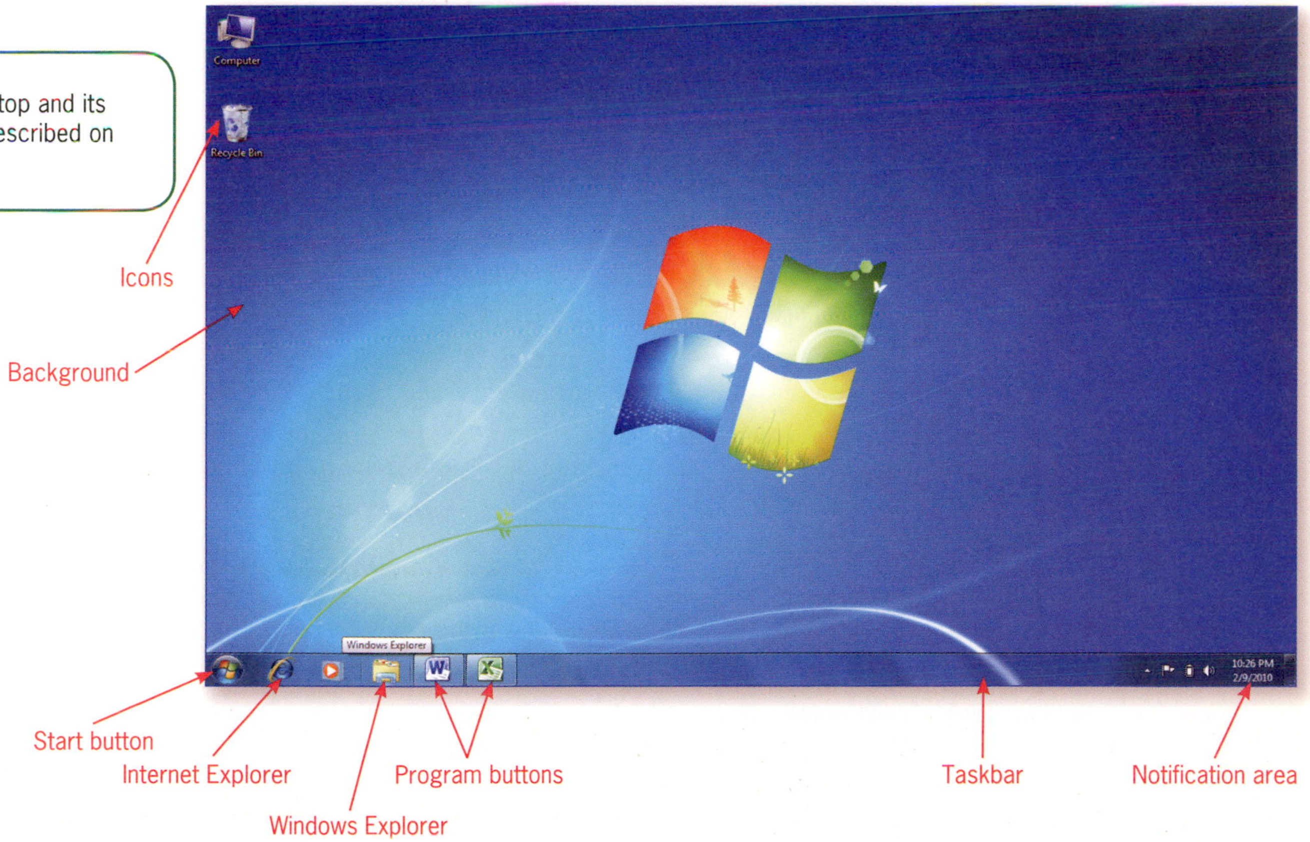

WINDOWS DESKTOP COMPONENTS

The illustration on the previous page shows the default *Windows* 7 Aero desktop. The Aero theme has a semitransparent glass design that gives a three-dimensional appearance. In order to see the graphical enhancements of the Aero theme, your computer hardware and version of *Windows* 7 must support it. Your screen may have the *Windows* 7 Basic theme.

Read the description of each component and hover the mouse over each object to display the ScreenTip that identifies each element.

- *Taskbar.* The taskbar displays across the bottom of the screen and contains the elements listed below.
    - *Start button.* Click the Start button to display the Start menu. The Start menu provides access to programs and files on your computer.
    - *Program and file buttons.* Buttons display for the programs that are open or pinned to the taskbar and allow you to switch between them easily. The illustration shows that *Internet Explorer, Windows Explorer, Word,* and *Excel* either are open or have been pinned to the taskbar so that they remain on the desktop.
    - *Notification area.* The notification area provides helpful information, such as the date and time and the status of the computer. When you plug in a USB drive, *Windows* displays an icon in the notification area letting you know that the hardware is connected.
- *Icons and Shortcuts.* Icons, small pictures representing certain items, may be displayed on the desktop. The Recycle Bin, which represents a wastepaper basket, displays when *Windows* is installed. Other icons and shortcuts may be added.
- *Background.* The default background is the *Windows* logo on a blue background. The background can be changed or customized to include a personal picture or a company logo.

START MENU

The Start menu enables you to access all programs, documents, and other computer resources. The programs listed in the left pane of the Start menu vary depending on which programs you have used recently. However, all programs can be located by clicking All Programs. The right pane contains links to files and resources on your computer. One of the key links that will be useful is Help and Support. Note that the Shut down button is also located on the Start menu.

To display the Start menu, click the Start button. The Start menu is illustrated on the next page. Review the callouts on the illustration on the next page.

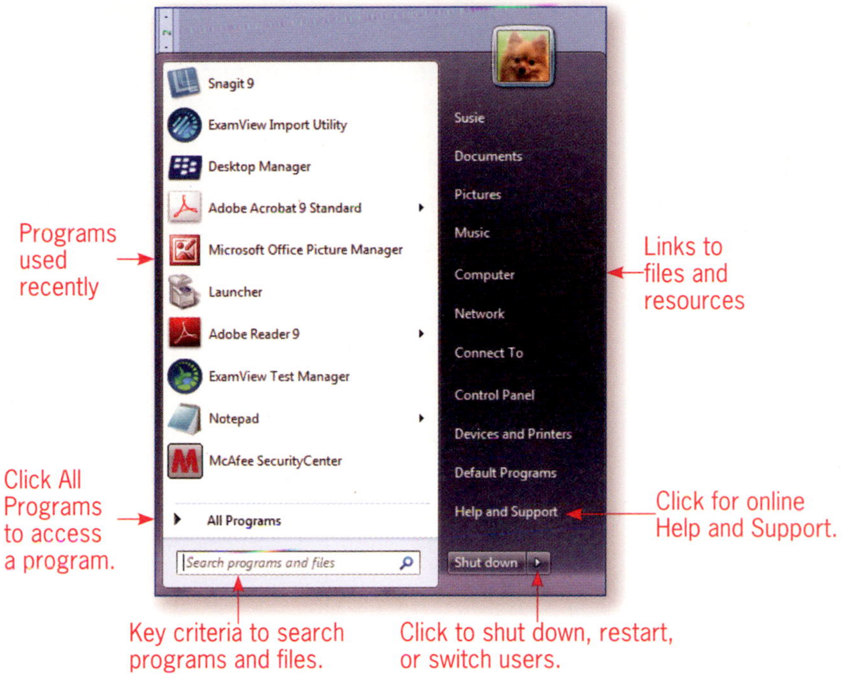

TIP

You will be able to access both the Help files stored on your computer and those stored on the Microsoft website if your computer is connected to the Internet.

WINDOWS 7 HELP AND SUPPORT

The fastest way to get help is to key a word or phrase in the Search Help box and tap ENTER; all the Help pages that contain the word or phrase will display. You can also click the Browse Help topics link and then click an item in the contents listing of subject headings that appear. Some subject headings contain Help topics within a subheading. Click the Help topic to open it, and click the subheading to narrow your search.

COMPUTER DRIVES

You will be working with auxiliary drives, including CD/DVD and universal serial bus (USB) flash drives. USB flash drives vary in size and shape and can hold gigabytes of information. They are also called thumb drives, memory keys, pen drives, and key drives. The USB drive needs to be plugged into a USB port in order for the computer to read the drive. Your computer may have several USB ports.

To access drives on your computer:

1. Click the Start button to display the Start menu.
2. Click Computer in the right pane to view the drives and storage devices connected to your computer.

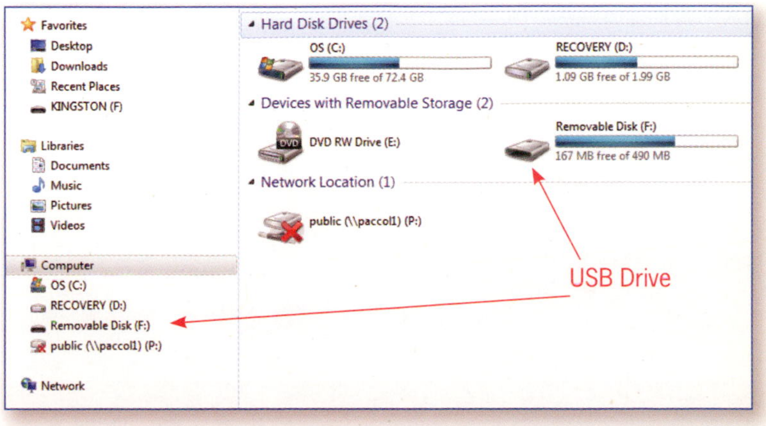

Section 2 | File Management

WINDOWS EXPLORER

Windows Explorer is a file management program provided with *Windows 7* Accessories. In the previous section, *Windows Explorer* was shown pinned to the taskbar. If your computer does not have it pinned to the taskbar, you can access *Windows Explorer* by right-clicking the Start button and selecting Open *Windows Explorer*.

LIBRARIES

When *Windows Explorer* opens it displays four libraries—Documents, Music, Pictures, and Video as shown in the illustration below.

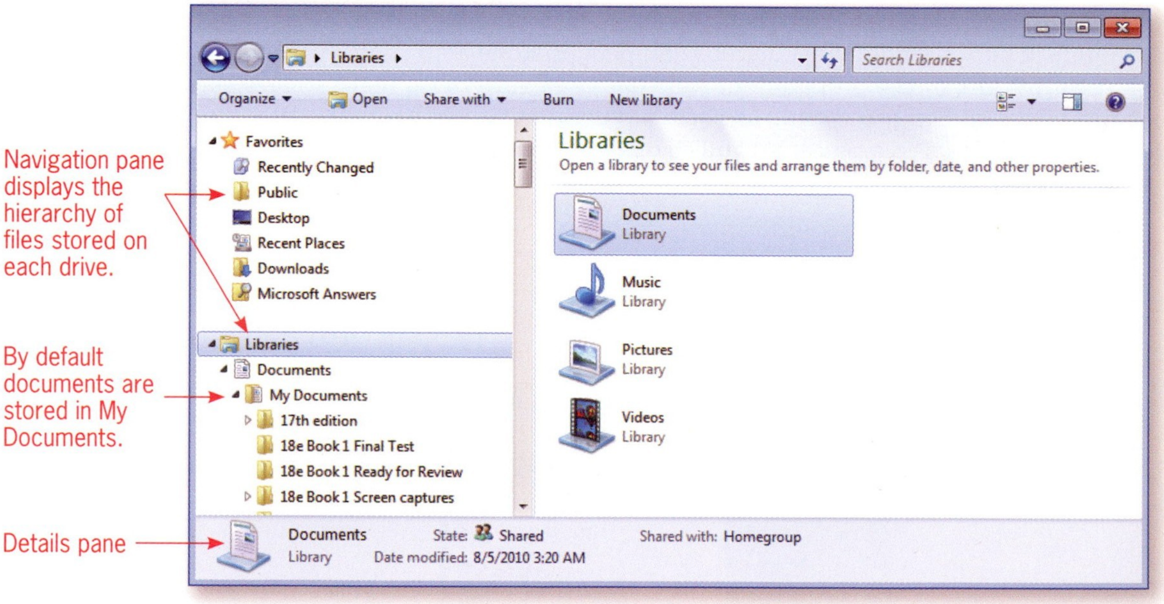

DOCUMENT MANAGEMENT

A logical system for storing documents enables you to locate and retrieve the documents when you need them. *Keyboarding Pro* stored your files in a logical system for you. However, if you were not using Keyboarding Pro, think how you could structure files for your Keyboarding class so that you could locate them quickly and easily. Your class has four major sections: Module 1, Module 2, Applying Keyboarding Skill, and Reference Guide. Applying Keyboarding Skill had four subsections: Numeric Keypad, Word Processing, Communication Skills, and Web-Based Computing. Having a folder for each would make it easy to locate and retrieve files.

FOLDER STRUCTURE

Note the file structure in *Windows Explorer* if you set up a folder for each section of the Keyboarding Class and subfolders for the Apply Keyboarding Skills section. Files relating to each of these areas would be stored in the appropriate folder.

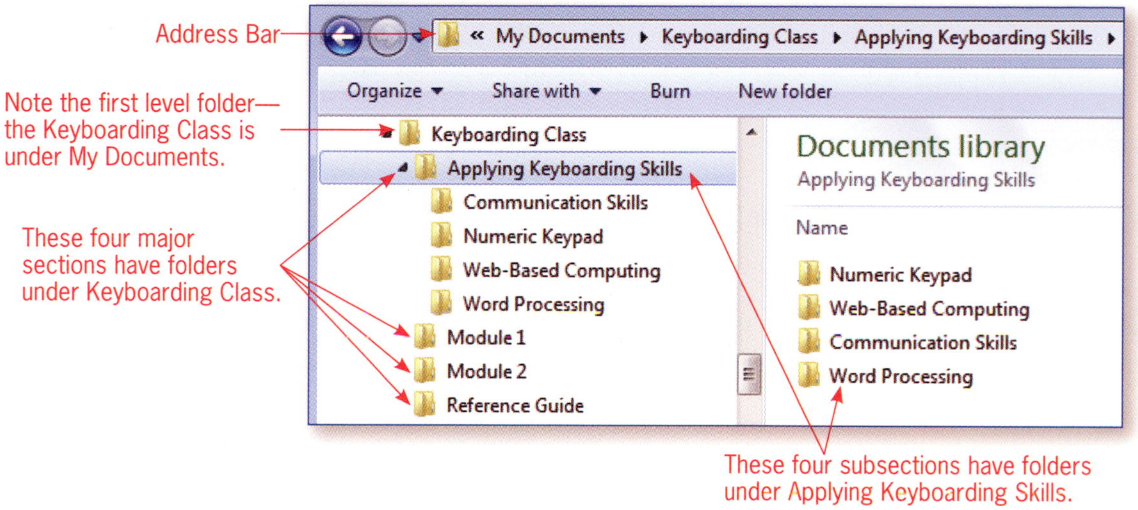

FOLDER ADDRESSES

A folder is a location for storing files or other folders. The Address Bar shows the location of the folders. Compare the address bar in the illustration above in which the folders are saved in My Documents on the hard drive OS (C:) and the illustration below in which the folders are saved on a USB (flash) drive.

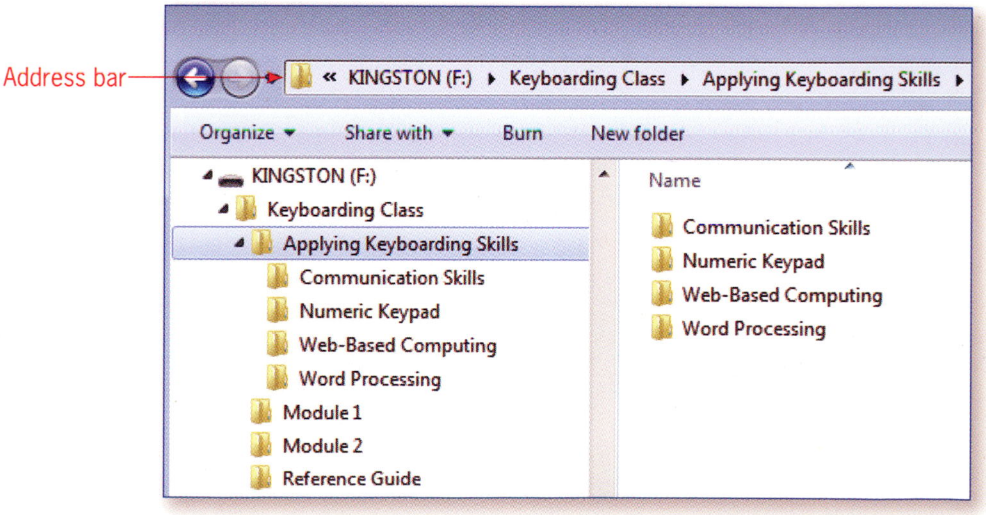

In the Address bar, each level of the hierarchy is separated with a ▸ symbol; the highest level folder displays at the left side of the Address bar. The ▸ symbol indicates the next lower level.

NAMING CONVENTIONS

The names given to both folders and files should be logical and should reflect the content of the folder or file. The names of folders are usually keyed with initial capital letters. The names of files are typically keyed using lowercase.

Filenames can be up to 255 characters long (but in practice you won't use filenames that long). In addition, the following symbols cannot be used in a filename: \/ : * ? “ , . The descriptive name is followed by a period (.), which is used to separate the descriptive name from the file extension. The file extension is three or four letters that follow the period. When renaming a file, do not delete or change file extensions as this may cause problems opening the file.

WORKING WITH FOLDERS AND FILES

Effective file management involves a number of tasks including creating folders, renaming folders and files, and copying, moving, and deleting folders and files. These tasks can be accomplished using *Windows Explorer* or using the Save As dialog box in applications such as *Word*, *Excel*, and *PowerPoint*. *Windows Explorer* is used for the following instructions.

To create a folder or subfolder:

1. In the Navigation pane, click the drive that is to contain the new folder. If a subfolder is desired, highlight the folder that will contain the new folder.

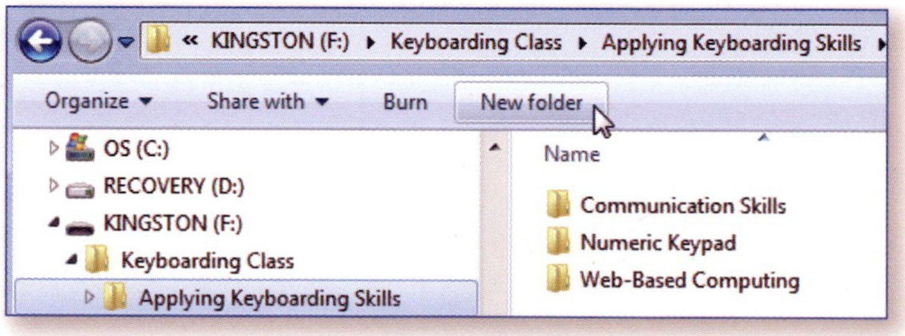

2. Click the New folder button to display a new folder.
3. Key the name of the new folder and tap ENTER.

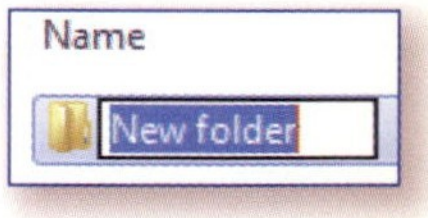

To copy a file or folder:

1. Highlight the file or folder that is to be copied. Click Organize and then click Copy.

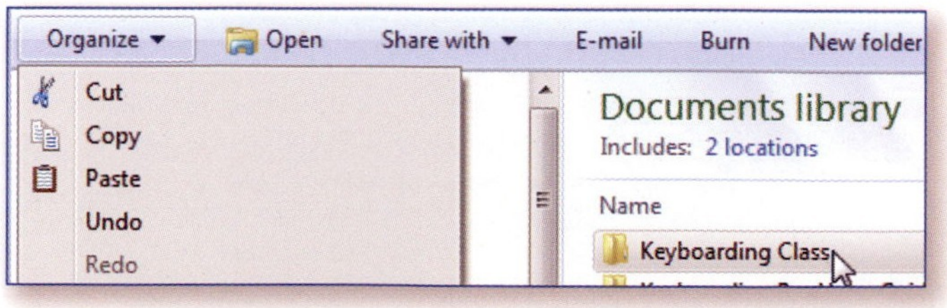

2. Navigate to the desired location, such as a flash drive, and click the icon.
3. Click Organize and then click Paste.

To rename a file or folder:

1. Right-click the file or folder icon.
2. Left-click Rename from the Shortcut menu.
3. Key the new name and tap ENTER.

To move a file or folder:

1. Highlight the file or folder that is to be moved and click Organize.

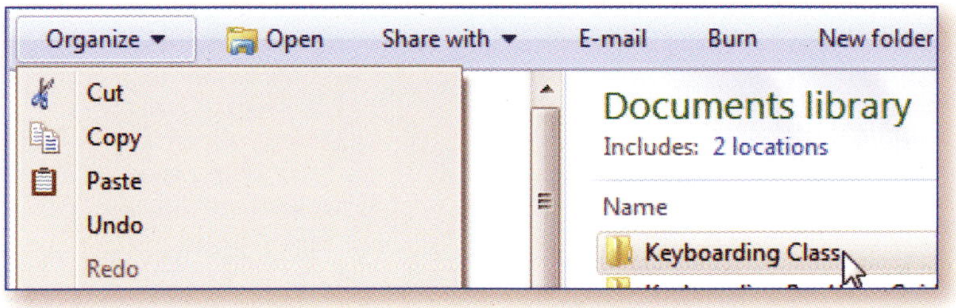

2. Click Cut.
3. Navigate to the desired location, such as a flash drive, and click the icon.
4. Click Organize and then click Paste.

TIP

You can also access the Cut, Copy, and Delete commands by selecting the filename; then right-click and choose the desired command from the menu.

To delete a file or folder:

1. Highlight the file or folder that is to be deleted.
2. Click Organize and then click Delete.
3. The Delete Folder dialog box displays to confirm the Delete request. Click Yes.

Note: Deleting a file removes it from its current location and sends it to the Recycle Bin; the file remains there until the Bin has been emptied.

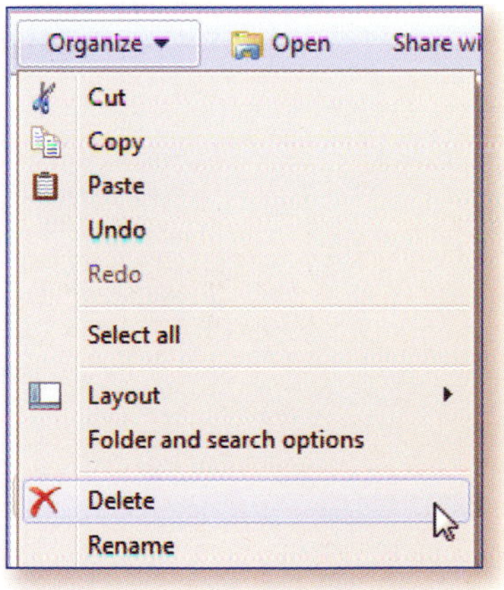

RECYCLE BIN

The Recycle Bin provides temporary storage for deleted files. If you accidentally delete a file, you can select the file and click Restore this item. To permanently remove all files, click Empty the Recycle Bin.

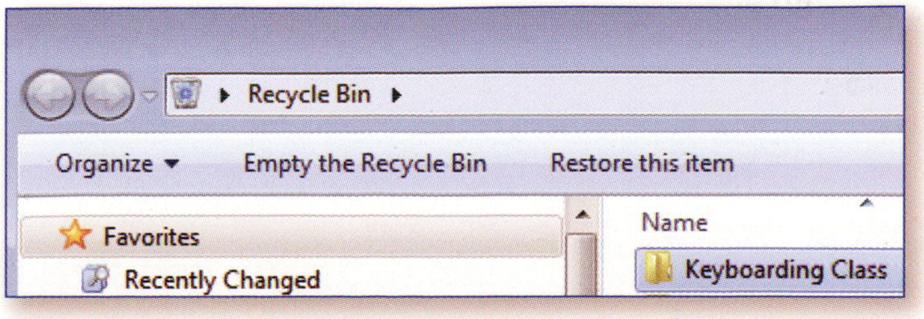

Index